Rodulfo González

THE BOLERO IN LATIN AMERICA

First published by Aussie Trading 2024
Copyright © 2024 by Rodulfo González
All rights reserved.
No part of this publication may be reproduced, stored or transmitted in any form or by any means, electronic, mechanical, photocopying, recording, scanning or otherwise without written permission from the publisher. It is illegal to copy this book, publish it on a website, or distribute it by any other means without permission.
Rodulfo Gonzalez has no responsibility for the persistence or accuracy of URLs of external or third-party Internet websites referenced in this publication and does not warrant that the content of such websites is, or will remain, accurate or appropriate.
The names used by companies to distinguish their products are often claimed as trademarks. All trademarks and product names used in this book and on its cover, trade names, service marks, trademarks are trademarks of their respective owners. The publishers and the book are not associated with any products or suppliers mentioned in this book. None of the companies or organizations referenced in the book have endorsed it.
Library of Congress Catalog
Name: Rodulfo González, 1935-
ISBN: 979-8-3306-1197-3 (paperback)
ISBN: 979-8-3306-1196-6 (e-book)
ISBN: 979-8-3306-1198-0 (hardcover)
First edition
Layout and Translation by Juan Rodulfo
Cover art by Guaripete Solutions
Production: CENTRO DE INVESTIGACIONES CULTURALES DEL ESTADO NUEVA ESPARTA (CICUNE)
cicune@gmail.com
Printed in the USA

cicune.org

The Bolero in Latin America

Table of Content

FOREWORD	**13**
CUBA	**17**
Xiomara Alfaro	17
Benny Moré	18
Orlando Contreras	19
Celia Cruz	20
La Sonora Matancera	21
Trío La Rosa	22
Trío Matamoros	23
Miguel Matamoros	24
Barbarito Diez	25
Rolando Laserie	26
Antonio Machín	26
Omara Portuondo	28
Elena Burke	29
Pedro Junco Jr.	30
César Portillo de la Luz	30
José Antonio Méndez García	31
Frank Domínguez	32
Ernesto Lecuona	33
Gonzalo Roig	34
Rodrigo Prats	35
COSTA RICA	**37**
Ray Tico	37
Francisco "Kiko" Barahona	37
Otto Vargas	38
Ricardo Mora	39
Jorge Duarte	40
The 8 great Costa Rican boleros	40
ECUADOR	**43**
Julio Jaramillo	43
Olimpo Cárdenas	43
Segundo Bautista	44
Lucho Bowen	44
Julio César Villafuerte	45

BOLIVIA ... 47
Los Genios ... 48

BRASIL ... 51
Altemar Dutra ... 51
Miltinho ... 51
Roberto Carlos ... 52
Simone ... 52
Chico Buarque ... 53
Lindomar Castilho ... 54
Los Indios Tabajaras ... 54
Nana Caymmi ... 55
Orquesta Serenata Tropical ... 56
Románticos de Cuba ... 56

COLOMBIA ... 57
Charlie Zaa ... 57
Faustino Arias ... 57
José Barros ... 58
Santander Díaz ... 58
Rafael Mejía ... 59
Lucho Bermúdez ... 59
Jaime R. Echavarría ... 60
Jorge Añez ... 60
Nelson Pinedo ... 61
Álvaro Dalmar ... 61
Oscar Fajardo ... 62
Claudia de Colombia ... 63
Tito Cortez ... 63

REPÚBLICA DOMINICANA. ... 65
Alberto Beltrán ... 65
Rafael Bullumba Landestoy ... 66
Papá Molina ... 66
Mario de Jesús ... 67
Héctor Acosta ... 68
Jackeline Estévez ... 68
Francis Santana ... 69
Luis Kalaff ... 69
Lope Balaguer ... 70

PANAMÁ 71
Ricardo Fábrega 71
Carlos Eleta Almarán 71
Arturo "Chino" Hassan 71
Martina Andrión 72
Rubén Blades 72
Avelino Muñoz 72

NICARAGUA 73
Rafael Gastón Pérez 73
Danny Tercero 74
First International Bolero Festival 74

PARAGUAY 77
Classic boleros sound today at the Municipal Theater 77
The Three South Americans 77
Luis Guitarra 78

EL SALVADOR 79
Álvaro Torres is 79

CHILE 81
Ginette Acevedo 81
Rosamel Araya 81
Lucho Gatica 82
Palmenia Pizarro 82
Antonio Prieto 83
Los Ángeles Negros 84

PERÚ 87
Los Pasteles Verdes 87
Pedro Otiniano 88
Lucho Barrios 88
Trío "Los Morunos" 90
Los Hermanos Castro 91
Johnny Farfán 91
Iván Cruz 92
Gaby Zevallos 92
Guiller 93

ARGENTINA 95

CARLOS ARGENTINO	95
MANUELA BRAVO	96
HORACIO CASARES	96
MARIO CLAVELL	97
ALBERTO CORTEZ	97
LEO MARINI	98
CHICO NOVARRO	99
EDUARDO FARREL	100
RAÚL CARRELL	100
PALITO ORTEGA	101
DANIEL RIOLOBOS	102
ELIO ROCA	103
SANDRO	103
ROBERTO YANÉS	104
PUERTO RICO	**107**
JOHNNY ALBINO	107
CHUCHO AVELLANET	107
HERNANDO AVILÉS	108
BOBBY CAPÓ	109
CHEO FELICIANO	109
CHARLIE FIGUEROA	110
DANIEL SANTOS	110
JOSÉ LUIS MONERÓ	111
CARMEN DELIA DIPINÍ	112
VIRGINIA LÓPEZ	113
RAFAEL HERNÁNDEZ	113
PEDRO FLORES	114
TITO RODRÍGUEZ	115
JOSÉ FELICIANO	116
DANNY RIVERA	116
RAFAEL MUÑOZ Y SU ORQUESTA	118
LOS TRÍOS	118
GUATEMALA	**121**
CÉSAR DE GUATEMALA	121
UNA TARDE DE TRÍOS Y BOLEROS	123
BOLERO CONCERT WITH THE NATIONAL CHOIR OF GUATEMALA AND THE LOS PRÍNCIPES TRIO	123
RICARDO ARJONA	124

MÉXICO 127

Juan Arvizu 127
Agustín Lara 128
Pedro Vargas 128
Toña La Negra 129
María Victoria 130
Consuelo Velásquez 130
Pedro Infante 131
José Alfredo Jiménez 131
Joaquín Pardavé 132
Alfonso Ortiz Tirado 133
Juan Gabriel 133
Ana Gabriel 134
Javier Solís 135
María Grever 136
Néstor Chayres 136
Guty Cárdenas 137
Chucho Martínez Gil 138
Marco Antonio Muñiz 138
Vicente Fernández 139
Antonio Aguilar 140
Gabriel Ruiz Galindo 141
Manuel Esperón 141

VENEZUELA 147

Lorenzo Herrera 147
Alfredo Sadel 148
Elisa Soteldo 149
Mirla Castellanos 150
Graciela Naranjo 151
Conny Méndez 151
Rafa Galindo 152
Rosalinda García 153
Eduardo Lanz 153
Guillermo Castillo Bustamante 154
María Luisa Escobar 155
Felipe Pirela 156
Luis Cruz 157
Simón Díaz 158
Ítalo Pizzolante 159

René Rojas 160
Héctor Cabrera 161
Marco Tulio Maristany 162
Mario Suárez 162
Rosa Virginia Chacín 163
María Teresa Chacín 164
Estelita del Llano 165
José Luis Rodríguez 165

THE AUTHOR **169**

REFERENCES **175**

FOREWORD

Between 1935 and 1965, the bolero dominated the Latin American musical spectrum. It was first promoted by radio and live programs, then by 78, 46 and 33 RPM records called acetates, then by film and finally by television.

It came from Spain to Cuba with characteristics different from those of today and from there it passed to Mexico, which, first by means of acetate, and then through films, to other Latin American countries, especially the Dominican Republic, Venezuela and Puerto Rico.

Initially, the bolero would be accompanied by guitar trios, quartets, quintets and sextets, then by the great tropical orchestras such as the Sonora Matancera in Cuba, the Billo's Caracas Boys in Venezuela and the Rafael Muñoz Orchestra of Puerto Rico and finally by the true symphony orchestras.

There are several subgenres of the bolero, namely: rhythmic bolero, cha-cha-cha bolero, mambola bolero, son bolero, vallenato bolero, ranchero bolero, cantinero bolero, bachata, filin and moruno bolero, among others.

The bolero is the popular musical genre that best expresses the romanticism of the Latin American people. Whether for love or heartbreak, the bolero serves to express feelings with precision. Its cult on the continent led to it being the only genre with a nickname: announcers often call it "His Majesty" or "Mr. Bolero." The bolero is a musical offspring of the Spanish contradanza. The bolero expert Tania Ruiz points out that the bolero was brought to America via Havana by Hispanic musicians who performed flamenco songs and who progressively mixed them with African rhythms and native sounds that they called habaneras, which they later reinforced with the incorporation of troubadours or singers, so called because they performed their own creations.

In turn, Manuel Felipe Sierra suggests in the prologue he wrote to the work Boleroterapia (2003: P. 7), originally by Humberto Márquez, that the bolero was born in 1883, when

José Pepe Sánchez composed "Tristezas" in Santiago de Cuba, becoming a kind of father of the bolero, although his profession was that of a tailor. According to that source: "In fact, the most conspicuous representatives of the trova were the Cubans José (Pepe) Sánchez and Nicolás Camacho, who were responsible for spreading the bolero across the seas, through Yucatán, Mexico, where they sowed the passion for that musical style due to the numerous artistic tours they made at the end of the 19th century."

Aldemaro Romero, for his part, states that the bolero had its origins in Spain during the 16th century. And although "it is true that the bolero is of Cuban origin, it is also true that its popularization throughout the Caribbean and, later, throughout Latin America, is due to the Mexicans", because: "In fact, the feeling that it inspired was planted in the Aztec soul when the composers Guty Cárdenas (1905-1932) and Agustín Lara (1900-1970) began to write their beautiful compositions, which were performed by Juan Arvizu, Pedro Vargas, Alfonso Ortiz Tirado and Néstor Chayres, who turned the bolero into a style that would become established throughout Latin America, until it became popular during its Golden Age, which could be located between 1925 and 1965."

On August 18, 2013, José Fefo Pérez wrote regarding the history of the bolero that it is lost in time "as far back as 1792, but it was not until 1902 when the rhythmic bolero appeared," which began "its transformation."

This author recognized that the bolero, indeed, "was born in Cuba after this country achieved its independence, precisely in Santiago de Cuba, according to some historians, with the bolero "Tristezas," by José Pepe Sánchez in 1886," in such a way that "Countries such as Puerto Rico, Mexico, Venezuela, the Dominican Republic and Colombia adopted the bolero, managing to popularize it throughout Latin America, which allowed the appearance of other bolero subgenres."

The author added that "In the first half of the 20th century, the bolero began its first significant change. Dance orchestras included the bolero as part of their obligatory repertoire," and "obviously, a new challenge for the musical arranger began, given the inclusion of instruments that until then were used only in symphonic string orchestras, because a distinction must be made. The charanga uses one or two violins and the transverse flute, but the bolero opened the strings to three or four violins and expanded the harmony with trumpets, saxophones and the trombone." And he observed: "It is important that the bolero became so sublimated those productions began to be made in theaters and concert halls to present recitals exclusively of boleros."

It should be noted that, according to some scholars, "the death of Carlos Gardel in 1935 left the tango without its most outstanding interpreter and encouraged the expansion of the bolero."

Although all scholars agree in pointing to Spain as the source of the bolero

But, although it was established throughout Latin America, it shares only the name with the Spanish bolero. In addition, the Spanish bolero was practiced in a specific region of Spain, while the Cuban one spread throughout Latin America.

What is a bolero?

Ignacio Veles Pareja in "El Diván del Bolero" pointed out in this regard: "It is said that the bolero is a defeatist, pessimistic music and verse that induces melancholy, but this is true in part because there are many kinds of boleros: of exaltation, of searches, reproaches, melancholy, and even songs to cities and religions."

And he added: "As a composer I can affirm that, in a certain way, with some exceptions, it is very difficult to write a bolero or a poem without there being a connection with the story being told." He clarified, however, that "there are many composers who can write on commission," but "the final result is never the best and among those exceptions is another prolific Puerto Rican composer, Tite Curet Alonso, who had an amazing talent for doing this work," of whom "it is said that on occasions he was asked to compose a song for X or Y singer and in a matter of a moment he would get it." Indeed, he composed "Anacaona" for Cheo Feliciano, "La Tirana" for La Lupe, "Tiemblas" for Tito Rodríguez and many more.

Fortunately, the bolero came to stay permanently in Latin America because it has many ways of reproducing itself culturally, through festivals and events such as Valentine's Day and Mother's Day or bolero groups that perform in theaters, clubs, stadiums, concert halls or in open spaces such as squares, streets and protected avenues.

To a greater or lesser degree, the bolero, which has the gift of immortality, is present in all Latin American countries, both in popular settings and in academic halls.

We recognize the existence of many exclusions in this monograph, which would require a large research team to work in each country to avoid, with the purpose of investigating each regional reality and thus achieving the clearest possible picture of Latin American bolero music.

I have worked alone, tying up loose ends to develop at least one reference that leads to more in-depth research studies.

CUBA

In this country, scholars of popular music place the origin of the first bolero, "**Tristezas**", by the troubadour *José "Pepe" Sánchez*. They differ with regard to the year of his birth, since some say that it was in 1883, the birth of the aforementioned bolero whose exact name was "**Me entristeces, mujer**" and others that it occurred in 1886.

That historical figure was born in Santiago de Cuba on March 19, 1856, and died on January 3, 1918.

He had no academic musical training, worked as a tailor and played guitar.

He also authored, among others, the songs "**Pobre artista**", "**Rosa I**", "**Rosa II**", "**Rosa III**", "**Elvira**", "**Cuando la expresión de tu canto**", "**Cuba, mi patria querida**", "**Caridad**", "**Adán y Eva**", "**Esperanza**", "**Redondilla**", "**Ángeles**", "**Nature**" and "**Hymn to Maceo**", etc.

From Cuba, via Yucatán, he traveled to Mexico, which would be in charge of disseminating it to the rest of Latin America through records and the cinema that gave way to the great orchestras and trios as part of the film.

Xiomara Alfaro, singer who was born in Havana on May 22, 1930 and died in Cape Coral, Florida, United States, on June 24, 2018.

She covered an entire stage of Cuban and Latin American popular song, emerged from the contest he won on a radio station in his country and began his artistic career in musical revues and cabaret shows.

She recorded more than 28 and performed numerous shows in various countries around the world.

The bolero "**Siboney**" by maestro Ernesto Lecuona was very popular in his voice, and the interpretation that the author liked the most.

Her discography includes, among others, the albums "**Besos en mis sueños**", "**Recordar es vivir**", "**Xiomara Alfaro en gira**", "**Xiomara Alfaro en Nueva York**", "**¡No puedo ser feliz!**", "**Recuerdos de Cuba**" and "**El Ruiseñor trina de nuevo**".[i]

Benny Moré is the stage name of the singer and composer *Bartolomé Maximiliano Moré Gutiérrez*, who was born in Santa Isabel de las Lajas on August 24, 1919, and died in Havana on February 19, 1963.

He was known as "***El Bárbaro del Ritmo***" and "***El Sonero Mayor de Cuba***".

He was a master in all genres, but he particularly excelled in son montuno, mambo and bolero.

He learned to play the guitar in his childhood and made his first instrument at the age of six, with a board and a spool of thread.

In 1935, he was part of his first musical group and the following year he moved to Havana, after six months he returned to his hometown.

In 1940 he returned to Havana and had his first success by winning a contest on the CMQ radio station, which had a program called **the Supreme Court of Art**, whose winners were hired and given the possibility of recording and singing their songs. That triumph allowed him to get his first stable job with the "**Cauto**" **Ensemble**, and also to sing successfully on the CMZ radio station with the "**Fígaro**" **Sextet**. In 1944 he made his debut on radio station 1010 with the "**Cauto**" Quartet.

Later he was part of the **Matamoros Trio**, with which he traveled to Mexico in June 1945 and there he stayed as part of the **Dueto Fantasma** and recording with the RCA Victor record company the songs "**Me voy pal pueblo**" and "**Desdichado**", together with the Mariano Mercerón orchestra.

With Dámaso Pérez Prado he recorded the songs "**Babarabatiri**", "**Guanabacoa**", "**Locas por el mambo**", "**Viejo cañengo**", "**El suave**", "**Que cinturita**", "**María Cristina**" and "**Pachito eché**", among others.

In Mexico he began to be known as "***The Prince of Mambo***".

In April 1952 he returned to Cuba, where he was practically unknown. "**Bonito y sabroso**" was his first recording in his native country and his first hit. Later he was part of the orchestra of Ernesto Duarte Brito, with which he recorded the famous bolero "**Cómo fue**".

Sometime later he founded La Banda Gigante, which between 1954 and 1955 became immensely popular. Between 1956 and 1957 he toured Venezuela, Jamaica, Haiti, Colombia, Panama, Mexico and the United States, where he performed at the Oscars ceremony.

His last presentation took place on Sunday, February 17, 1963, in Palmira, Cienfuegos, a few kilometers from Santa Isabel de las Lajas, his hometown.ii

Orlando Contreras was the stage name of singer Orlando *González* Soto, who was born in Havana on May 22, 1930, and died in Medellín, Colombia on February 9, 1994.

It was called by its fans "***The Romantic Voice of Cuba***".

He was part of the Arly *Valdés trio*, the **Casino Ensemble** and the Neno *González orchestra*, with which he recorded a successful album.

She later became a soloist.

In 1965 he traveled to the United States and between 1966 and 1970 he worked on a Portuguese tourist boat.

One of his greatest hits was "**Mi Corazonada**", by *José Fernández Pérez*.

His repertoire also included, among other songs that made him famous in Cuba and Latin America, the titles "En un beso la vida", "**Sin egoísmo**", "**Difficult**", "**Amarga decepción**", "**Por borracha**", "**Por un handful de oro**", "**Dónde tu irás**", "**Muerto en vida**", "**Dolor de hombre**", "**Que murmuren**", "**Un amigo mío**", "**Amigo de qué**", "**Yo estoy desengañado**", "**Arráncame la vida**", "**Egoísmo**", "**Esta tu canción**", "**Sé muy bien que vendrás**" and "**Corazón de Madera**".[iii]

Celia Cruz was the stage name of the singer *Úrsula Hilaria Celia de la Caridad Cruz Alfonso*, who was born in Havana on October 21, 1925 and died in Fort Lee (United States) on July 16, 2003.

She was called by her fans *"The Queen of Salsa"* and *"The Guarachera of Cuba"*.

Throughout his career he interpreted and popularized internationally the son, son montuno, guaguancó, rumba, guaracha and bolero.

She was the vocalist of the **Sonora Matancera** orchestra and won numerous awards, including two **Grammys** and three **Latin Grammys**.

The expression *¡Azúcar!* that he used in his interpretations identified it.

He recorded with the labels Seeco Records, Tico Records, Fania - Vaya Label, Bárbaro Records, RMM Records, Sony Music Entertainment, Universal Music Latino, Cubanacan Recordss and Elektra / Asylum Records.

Among the boleros he performed are the titles **"Cuando Salí De Cuba"**, **"Perdón"**, **"Vieja luna"**, **"Y volveré"**, **"No Me Hables De Amor"**, **"Esperaé"**, **"Cuando Estoy Contigo"**, **"Preferí Perderte"**, "Extraño Amor", **"Pquiero Tu Amor"**, **"Falsía"**, "Desencanto", **"Ya Lo Puede Decir"**, **"Tengo Un Carñito"**, **"Te Busco"**, **"Bravo"**, **"No Me Vaya A Engañar"**, **"Mi Desperación"**, **"Encantado De La Vida"**, **"Bolero"**, **"Me Recuerdo Gracias A Ti"** and **"Soy"**.[iv]

La Sonora Matancera is an orchestra born in Matanzas that, in addition to son cubano, salsa, guaracha, son montuno, guaguancó, mambo, conga, cha, cha, cha and other popular genres, performed rhythmic bolero, bolero moruno, bolero mambo, son bolero, bolero tango, bolero, bolero beguine, bolero, bolero guapachá, bolero afro, bolero bon-bon and bolero guajiro.

On January 12, 1924, under the initiative of **Valentín Cané** and precisely in his house, the group was formed under the name of **Tuna Liberal**, at the request of a local political party of the same name that requested its formation to liven up its meetings and rallies. In its origins it was a group in which the strings prevailed since it was the time of the rise of the "***Son***", and for these four acoustic guitars were required.

Among the bolero singers who were part of the orchestra are **Daniel Santos**, **Celia Cruz**, **Myrta Silva**, **Leo Marini**, **Miguelito Valdés**, **Bobby Capó**, **Nelson Pinedo**, Vicentico Valdés, **Alberto Beltrán**, **Johnny López**, Carlos Argentino, Celio González, **Carmen Delia Dipiní**, Olga Chorens, **Willy Rodríguez**, **Toña la Negra** and **Bienvenido Granda**, among the best known.

His 40 golden boleros are as follows: **"Total", "Quién será", "Dile que por mí no temá", "Todo me gusta de ti", "Cuando tú eres mía", "En el juego de la vida", "Dos almas", "Por dos caminos", "Amor sin esperanza", "Desesperación", "Tuya y más que tuya", "Although it costs me my life", "The earrings of the moon", "The prisoner", "Story of a love", "Morena", "That's better", "They deceived you heart", "Song of pain", "Christmas memories", "The 19th", "Without thinking about you", "In the palm of the hand", "In love", "Anguish", "Disgrace", "Wake of Love", "New York Lights", "Burn My Eyes", "Heart Without a Port", "Indecision",** "Copper Love", "One **Hundred Thousand Things", "It's All Over",** "When You Come Back With Me", "Amnesty", **"Me I live my life", "On the balcony that", "On the seashore"** and **"I only have a love".**

On June 15, 1960, the group left Cuba to fulfill a juicy contract it had in Mexico City, and did not return to its country.

In New York's Central Park, on July 1, 1989, was the celebration of the 54th anniversary of its founding.[v]

Trío La Rosa was a musical group that, in addition to performing guaracha, spread the bolero in Cuba and other Latin American countries.

It was created in Santiago de Cuba by Juan *Francisco de la Rosa*, its director, *Julio León* and *Juan Antonio Serrano*.

But in 1943 *Julio León* rehired him as director, arranger, second voice and accompanying guitar, with *Juan F. Serrano* first voice and minor percussion, and Francisco Jiménez Puentes, third voice and first guitar, who was soon replaced by *Juan Francisco Despaigne La Rosa*.

At that stage, in addition to their performances, they accompanied figures of the oriental trova.

He soon moved to Havana hired by the RHC and in 1947 they began to record for Panart.

In 1947 *Chago Rodrigo* and *Celso Vega* were invited to participate in some recordings for Panart.

The same thing happened the following year, The guest was *Luisa María Hernández* "**La India De Oriente**" who recorded "Contestación a por seguir tus huellas", her first album with that record label.

The bolero "**Amor que malo eres**" is successful and his recordings are already known throughout the Caribbean area.

Other hits were: "**La Fiesta de los Ratones**", "**Errante de un Amor**", "**Triste Camino**", "**Zancudo Patilargo**", "**Pegadita A Los Hombres**", "**Fue En La Cantina**", "**Mar y cielo**", "**Mi ruego de amor**", "**Acuérdame de ti**", "**Paloma caprichosa**", "**Blancas azucenas**" and "**The one that left**."[vi]

Trío Matamoros was a group founded in Santiago de Cuba on May 8, 1925 that, in addition to the bolero, performed other genres of popular music that were heard in various parts of the world.

Its founders were *Miguel Matamoros*, *Rafael Cueto* and *Siro Rodríguez*.

His music was at the time, and still is, one of the most genuinely popular syntheses of Cubanness.

The trio traveled to the United States for the first time in 1928, where they made their first recordings; in 1929 he went to Mexico; in 1930 to Santo Domingo, Dominican Republic, and in 1933, he toured Venezuela, Panama, Curaçao, Puerto Rico and Colombia, and in 1960 he appeared for the last time in the United States.

On his return to Cuba, after 35 years of intense artistic life, he disintegrated.

He performed for the last time for the Cuban people at the Chaplin Theater in Havana in early March 1960.

Its success is attributed to the creation, by *Miguel Matamoros*, of the bolero son.

Among his main boleros are "**Conciencia**", "**Mata y bebe**", "**Santiaguera**", "**Olvido**", "**Ruego de amor**", "**Noche triunfal**", "**Promesa**" and "**Luz que no alumbra**".[vii]

Miguel Matamoros was a singer, musician and composer who was born in Santiago de Cuba on May 8, 1894, and died in the same city on April 15, 1971. He created the bolero and founded the **Trío Matamoros**, along with *Siro Rodríguez* and *Rafael Cueto*.

His musical training was self-taught, although at the age of 15 he began to play the guitar in the key A Major taught to him by Ramón Navarro.

But the first musical instrument that marked him as a performer in the activities in which he participated was the harmonica and then the Chinese cornet, which he played at the request of *Rita Montaner* in one of her performances years later at the **Cabaret Montmartre**, when he was completely dedicated to artistic life.

At the age of 16 he composed his first musical piece: a bolero that he titled "**El Consejo**", and over time his compositions totaled almost 200, between that genre and sones, pasodobles, habaneras and polkas, among others.[viii]

Barbarito Diez, was the stage name of the singing musician, *Bárbaro Diez Junco*, who was born in Bolondrón on December 4, 1909 and died in Havana on May 6, 1995.

He was known as *"**The Golden Voice of Danzón**"*.

He was active from 1935 to 1985 and recorded with the Panart and EGREM labels.

He formed the trio "**Los Gracianos**" with the troubadour *Graciano Gómez* and the musician *Isaac Oviedo*, thus beginning his professional life.

From 1935, he joined as a solo voice in the orchestra of the Cuban conductor and arranger *Antonio María Romeu*.

With this orchestra, he performed danzones, sones and boleros for more than five decades.

When *Romeu* died on January 18, 1995, he assumed the direction of the group, which he renamed "**Barbarito Diez and his orchestra**".

He also founded the **Cuarteto Selecto**, with which he performed in the cabarets of the Havana bohemia of the forties.

It is good to point out, as the source consulted, that *"Although his style was always linked to danzón, in 1984 he recorded in Venezuela his only LP of boleros, accompanied by the guitars and voices of the Venezuelan group "**La Rondalla Venezolana**".*

The recording was made through an agreement between the Venezuelan company "Palacio de la Música" and the Cuban state record company EGREM, which had Diez exclusively.

On that album appear the boleros **"Frenesí"** and **"Idolatría"**.[ix]

Rolando Laserie, was the stage name of percussionist and singer *Rolando Laserie Rodríguez*, who was born in Mata, Villa Clara, on August 27, 1923 and died in Coral Gable, Florida, United States, on November 22, 1998.

He was known as *"El Guapo"* or *"El Guapachoso"*.

He learned to play the timpani at the age of 9 and performed sporadically as a percussionist in the **Municipal Band of Santa Clara**.

At the age of 20 he was part of the orchestra of **Arcaño y sus Maravillas**.

In 1946 he traveled to Havana and worked as a percussionist in the orchestra of the **Palau Brothers**.

Later he became timbalero and choir in **Benny Moré's Banda Gigante**.

An album of boleros recorded with the Gema record label had no repercussions.

In 1957 the bolero **"Mentiras tuyas"**, authored by *Mario Fernández Porta*, was defining in its way of singing, with colloquial incursions and dialogues.

Throughout his career he recorded more than thirty albums.

With the advent of the Cuban Revolution, he emigrated first to Caracas, Venezuela, and then to Miami, where he continued his career, counting on a good part of his audience.[x]

Antonio Machín was the stage name of the musician and singer *Antonio Abad Lugo Machín*, who was born in Sagua la Grande on February 11, 1903 and died in Madrid on August 4, 1977.

He became famous for the recreations he made of the songs "**El Manisero**", "**Dos gardenias**" and "**Angelitos negros**", among others.

"**El manisero**", which was recorded in 1930 accompanied by the Don *Azpiazu* orchestra for the RCA Víctor company of New York, was the first millionaire success in sales of Cuban music.

In 1911, the parish priest of his hometown made him sing on his main altar and on one occasion, on the occasion of a charity festival, he performed **Schubert's Ave Maria** on a chair, earning the applause of the entire population.

He moved to Havana in 1926, where he began as a soloist in the cafes, accompanied by guitarist *Miguel Zaballa*.

The reputation of the duo – *we read in Wikipedia, the free encyclopedia* – reached the ears of the Havana bourgeoisie, who no longer hesitated to hire them. By chance of fate he came to sing on a radio station where *Don Azpiazu coincided*, who hired him as the second singer of his orchestra. He would be, therefore, the first black singer to perform at the **Casino Nacional in Havana**, a place of the most racist and exclusionary bourgeoisie, already as a professional. Without leaving *Azpiazu*, he founded a sextet that made its first recordings in 1929 and from the media of the time, that is, the string victrolas and the radio that was beginning to develop. The success was immediate with "**Esos ojos verdes**", which was followed by **"El manisero"**. In 1930 he left Cuba, where he would not return until 1958.

In 1939 he settled in Spain, where he scored his first hit with "**Noche triste**", a melodic fox recorded with the Mihuras. The songs "**Cómo fue**", "**Moreno**" and "**Amor sincero**" were also hits.

However, his great success would come in 1947, with the Moorish song "**Angelitos negros**" turned into a bolero thanks to a musical arrangement.

His repertoire also included the boleros "**Madrecita**", "Toda una vida", "**Bésame mucho**", "No me vayas a engañar", "**Quizás, quizás, quizás**" and "**Dos gardenias**", among many others.

Two important composers in his career were the Cuban *Osvaldo Farrés* (author of songs such as **Madrecita, Toda una vida, No me vayas a engañar, Quizás, quizás, quizás, Ay de mí...**) and the Mexican *Consuelo Velázquez* (author of **Bésame mucho, Será por eso** and **Amar y vivir**). Special mention should be made of the only version by the Cuban *Isolina Carrillo*, which she turned into one of her greatest hits, "**Dos gardenias**".

In that country he recorded more than 60 albums and formed the "Cuarteto Machín".[xi]

Omara Portuondo is the stage name of singer *Omara Portuondo Péláez*, who was born in Havana on October 29, 1930.

She began his artistic career in 1945.

Interpreter of bolero, jazz, filin and son.

She is considered the maximum representative of the filin, a Cuban subgenre of the bolero.

Website: www.omaraportuondo.com

She began her artistic career in 1945 as a dancer at the Tropicana cabaret, where she teamed up with the famous dancer *Rolando Espinosa*.

In his beginnings he sang with a group that called itself **Loquibambla Swing**, and the style they played was a music

The Bolero in Latin America

that influenced jazz that later became known as feeling castellanizado filin.

In 1950 he was a member of the **Anacaona Orchestra**, and around 1952 with his sister Haydée, *Elena Burke* and *Moraima Secada*, he formed a vocal group led by the pianist *Aída Diestro*, called the **Las d'Aída Quartet that** lasted 15 years and in 1957 recorded an album for RCA Victor. The group toured extensively in America and shared the stage with *Édith Piaf, Pedro Vargas, Rita Montaner, Bola de Nieve and Benny Moré* and also served as accompanists for *Nat King Cole* when he performed at the Tropicana cabaret.

She was part of the **Aragón Orchestra**.

In 1959 he made his solo debut with the album Magia Negra.

She toured extensively, performing in France, Japan, Belgium, Finland and Sweden.

Her bolero repertoire included, among many others, **"Flor de amor"**, **"Nosotros"**, **"Camino del puerto"**.**A whole life**" and "**Ella y yo**".[xii]

Elena Burke was the stage name of the singer *Romana Elena Burke González*, who was born in Havana on February 28, 1928 and died in the same city on June 9, 2002.

In addition to bolero, he performed, beat, pop, son, romantic ballads and other genres.

She began his career working in radio at the end of the forties, at the **Supreme Court of Art**, where he signed his first contract with maestro *Orlando de La Rosa*.

She belonged to the group **Las Mulatas de Fuego**, the trio **Las Cancioneras** and the quartets of *Facundo Rivero, Orlando de La Rosa* and the pianist *Aída Diestro*.

Her repertoire included songs by Latin American composers and those of his country.

Among the numerous hits are the songs "**De mis recuerdos**", "**Y ya lo sé**", "**Lo material**", "**Duele**", "**Amor y solfeo**" (*Luis Rojas*), "**Ámame como soy**" and "**Mis 22 años**".

She recorded the albums Gemas de Navidad, Elena Burke canta a Marta Valdés, La Burke canta, Elena Burke canta a Juan Formell, A solas contigo and De lo que te has perdido.[xiii]

Pedro Junco Jr. is the name by which the pianist and composer *Pedro Buenaventura Jesús del Junco-Redondas* was known, who was born in Pinar del Río on February 22, 1930, and died in Havana on April 25, 1943.

His songs are the classic bolero "**Nosotros**", "**Estoy triste**", "**Soy como soy**", "**Me lo dijo el mar**", "**Quisiera**" and "**Tus ojos**".

In 1939 he obtained the title of piano teacher.

His bolero "**Nosotros**" was sung for the first time in February 1943 by the singer *Tony Chiroldes* on the Pinar del Río CMAB Radio Station.

Since then, it has been sung by more than 400 performers.

Minutes before he died, he heard the radio premiere of his bolero "*Soy como soy*" by singer *René Cabel*.[xiv]

César Portillo de la Luz is the name of the composer, singer and guitarist who was born in Havana on October 31, 1922 and died in the same city on May 4, 2013.

He was active from 1940 until the year of his death.

From the age of 19 he began singing accompanied by his guitar. He was among the promoters of the filin, a particular way of interpreting the bolero, with the influence of jazz,

"**Contigo en la distancia**" is the name of his best-known bolero, his authorship is also "**Tú mi delirio**", "**Sabrosón**", "**Noche cubana**", "**Realidad y Fantasía**" and "**Canción de un festival**".

Several of his songs have been performed, among others, by *Nat King Cole, Tito Rodríguez, Olga Guillot, Pedro Infante, Litto Nebbia, Tin Tan, José José, Pedro Vargas, Lucho Gatica, Fernando Fernández, Luis Miguel, Luis Mariano, Plácido Domingo, Christina Aguilera, Caetano Veloso, María Bethania, Astrid Gilberto* and the *London Symphony Orchestra*.[xv]

José Antonio Méndez García, was a composer, singer and guitarist who was born in Havana on June 10, 1927, and died in the same city on June 10, 1989. He is among the founders of the filin.

His compositions are internationally recognized.

In 1940 he appeared in **the Supreme Court of Art**, where he won the first prize with the corrido "**Cocula**"

In 1946 he wrote "**Por mi ceguedad**" and "**Novia mía**" and the following year the bolero "**La gloria eres tú**", popularized by *Toña la Negra* and *Pedro Infante*, who interpreted it in the Mexican film "**Dos tipos de cuidado**".

He was a member of the **Xochimilco** trio, and the **Loquibambia group**.

He also presided over the Musicabana publishing house, made up of filin cultists. In 1949 he traveled to Mexico, where he was already known for the recordings of "**La gloria eres tú**".

In 1955 he recorded for RCA Víctor, at the initiative of *Mario Rivera Conde*, artistic director of that record company, his first LP with his own songs and those of other composers.

The following year he traveled to Guatemala and from there returned to Mexico, where he composed in 1957, "**Si me comprendieras**", which *Lucho Gatica* recorded with the Sabre *Marroquín orchestra*.

These are other of his compositions: "**Por mi ceguedad**", "**Soy tan feliz**", "**Cemento, ladrillo y arena**", "**Como los otros**", "**Ese sentimiento que se llama amor**", "**Me faltabas tú**", "**Mi mejor canción**", "**Por nuestra cowardía**", "**Suffer more**", "**You, my divine love**", "**And decidete, my love**", "**Yesterday I saw her cry**", "**Love me and you will see**", "**Talk to me in front**", "**The last one I bring**" and "**Why do you doubt?**".[xvi]

Frank Domínguez is the stage name of singer, pianist and composer *Francisco Manuel Ramón Dionisio Domínguez Radeón*, who was born in Matanzas, on October 9, 1927, and died in Mérida, Yucatán, Mexico, on October 29, 2014. He obtained the nationality of that country.

He was a relevant figure in the filin movement.

He began practicing the piano at the age of 8. He graduated as a pharmacist at his father's wishes, but he never practiced the profession.

In 1958, he released his first album: Frank Domínguez sings his songs.

His most famous bolero, "**Tú me acostumbraste**", written in 1957, went around the world in the voices *of Los Tres Ases, Olga Guillot, Chavela Vargas, María Dolores Pradera, Pedro Vargas, Caetano Veloso, Doménico Modugno, Tom Jones, Mina, Gal Costa, María Bethania,*

Lola Flores, Los Sabandeños, Bambino, Luis Miguel, Sara Montiel, Gipsy Kings, Natalia Lafourcade, Omara Portuondo, Los Macorinos, Chucho Valdés, Andrea Bocelli and *Alex Ferreira*, among many others.

He also wrote the compositions "**Pedacito de cielo**", "'**How dare you?**", "**You will remember me**", "**Images**", "**Refuge in me**", "**How you dare**", "**My heart cried**", "**Piece of heaven**", "**Don't ask for impossibles**", "**If you want**", "**A little piece of heaven**", "**Moon Over Matanzas**", "**My Song to Havana**", "**Sad Goodbye Juventud**", "**Cuando No Te Veo Vida Mía**", "**El Jibarito**", "**La Rosa Ausente**" and "**Tu Mirar**".[xvii]

Ernesto Lecuona is the stage name of the pianist and singer-songwriter *Ernesto Sixto de la Asunción Lecuona Casado*, who was born in Guanabacoa on August 8, 1895 and died in Santa Cruz de Tenerife, Spain, on November 29, 1963.

He composed popular and academic music.

He gave his first recital at the age of 5, and at 13 he made his first composition, the march "**Cuba y América**" for concert band.

She graduated from the National Conservatory of Havana with a gold medal in acting when she was 16 years old.

He is considered one of the most outstanding Cuban musicians. His traces were recorded in popular and academic songs.

He has authored the classics of Cuban popular music "**Siboney**", "**Canto Carabalí**", "**La Comparsa**" and "**Malagueña**", among many other songs.

Among its most famous performers are the Mexican tenor **José Mojica**, the Spanish tenor **Alfredo Kraus**, the pianist **Huberal Herrera** and many others.

"**Siboney**", one of his best-known popular songs, composed on December 28, 1919 and published in 1928. Among the first performers are **Rita Montaner** and **Vicente Morín**, who sang it together on September 29, 1927 at the old Regina Theater in Havana.

She has also been performed by **Esther Borja**, **Xiomara Alfaro**, **Libertad Lamarque**, María América Samudio, **Nana Mouskouri**, the **Los Panchos trio**, **Alfredo Graus**, **Plácido Domingo**, **Connie Francis** and **Grace Moore**, among many others.

In 1942 Juan Orol made the film of the same name.

It is included in the soundtrack of the American films, **When You're in Love** directed by Robert Riskin in 1937, **2046** by Wong Kar-wai in 2004 and in **The Island** by Michael Bay in 2005.[xviii]

Gonzalo Roig is the stage name of musician and composer *Gonzalo Roig Lobo*, who was born in Havana on July 20, 1890, and died in the same city on June 13, 1970.

He founded several orchestras and was a pioneer of the symphonic movement in Cuba and one of the main composers who redefined Cuban zarzuela. He was also the founder of the **National Opera of Havana**, which he directed for some years, of the Society of Authors of Cuba, the National Federation of Authors of Cuba, the National Union of Authors of Cuba and the National Society of Authors of Cuba.

He graduated from the Havana Conservatory.

He composed other classics of Cuban popular music, the bolero "**Quiéreme mucho**" and "**Ojos brujos**", among many other songs. He is also the composer of the zarzuelas "**Cecilia Valdés**", "**La Habana de Noche**", "**La hija del sol**" and "**El clarín**".[xix]

Rodrigo Prats is the stage name of the composer, violinist, pianist and conductor Rodrigo *Ricardo Prats Llorens*, who was born in Sagua la Grande, province of Las Villas, on February 7, 1909 and died in Havana on September 15, 1980.

In 1924, at the age of 15, he composed the music for the well-known bolero "**Una rosa de Francia**". about the lyrics of a poem that **Gabriel Gravier**, a friend of the family, had given him. It was premiered by the popular singer **Fernando Collazo**.

In 1961, with his work "**Yo sí tumbo caña**", performed by the D'Aida quartet, he won the grand prize of the First Cuban Song Contest held in 1959.

Other songs of his authorship are the proclamations "**El churrero**", "**El tamalero**", "**El verdulero**" and "**El heladero**", among others; the boleros "**Una rosa de Francia**", already mentioned, "**Aquella noche**", "**Espero de ti**", "**Tú que no sabes mentir**", "**Creo que te quiero**", "**Eres rayo de sol**" and "**Miedo al desengaño**". Likewise, zarzuelas. "**Amalia Batista**", "**The Pearl of the Caribbean**", "**María Belén Chacón**", "**The Havana that returns**", "**Guamá**". and "**Soledad**".[xx]

COSTA RICA

The bolero arrived in this country at the beginning of the twentieth century and among the most important cultists are the names of **Ricardo Mora**, **Orlando Zeledón**, **Ray Tico**, **Jorge Duarte**, **Gilberto Hernández** and **Rafa Pérez**.

Ray Tico is the stage name used by the musician, singer and composer *Ramón Jacinto Herrera*, who was born in Limón on an unspecified date in 1928 and died on August 15, 2007.

He is considered an icon of Costa Rican popular music and was the only foreigner who was part of the Cuban "filin" movement, with which the bolero reached its maximum splendor.

It was in Cuba that he adopted his stage name.

He composed more than fifty songs, including the bolero "**Eso es imposible**", the work that lavished the most hits on him, "**Romance en La Habana**", "**México de luz y color**" "**Me quedo callado**".[xxi]

Francisco "Kiko" Barahona, musician and composer who was born on August 6, 1922, in Naranjo, Alajuela.

He was part of the orchestra led by **maestro Hugo Mariani** and in 1944 he formed the **Lubin Barahona Orchestra and his Knights of Rhythm**.

Among others, he has written the songs "**Noche azul**", "**En la distancia**", "**Volveré**", "**Dónde tú estés**", "**Un sueño de amor**" and "**Noche azul**".

"**Volveré**" was recorded by the Luis Alcaraz Orchestra, and "**Noche azul**", by Jorge Duarte.

He was a member of the aforementioned orchestra and of the orchestra conducted by Dámaso Pérez, with whom he performed in Japan.[xxii]

Otto Vargas, stage name of the saxophonist, arranger, composer and orchestra leader **Otto Vargas Rojas**, who was born in Alajuela on November 24, 1927, and died in the same town on February 3, 2017

His first musical instrument was a toy marimba.

He was a member of the "Toño" Solís Orchestra, Marimba Orchestra Costa Rica, of the Sanabria brothers, and of Saúl Menéndez. Rodolfo Guiadams and his Escuadrón del Ritmo and Gilberto Murillo's orchestra made their first recording, the single "**Solo quiero mirarte**" for the ARPA label, which was performed by **Rafa Pérez**.

At the end of 1958 he bought the rights to Gilberto Murillo's Orchestra and incorporated vocalist Gilberto Hernández, and renamed the group as: **Otto Vargas' Fabulosa**, which performed in the United States, Central America and the Caribbean.

That group alternated with Billo's Caracas Boys, El gran combo de Puerto Rico, La Sonora Matancera and La Sonora Santanera, among others.

From his inspiration came the songs "**Amor del Mar**", "**La Leyenda de tus ojos**" and "**Te esperaé**" (recorded by the trio Los Josefinos).

His orchestra ceased its activity in December 1996, with a balance of several 45 rpm albums and 18 LPs, among them the one entitled Otto Vargas y su Música y su Orquesta, constant of the songs "**Costa Rica**", "**Sólo quiero mirarte**", "**Para mis amigos**", "**Amor del mar**", "**Como un sueño", "Esta Navidad", "San José de Costa Rica", "Have to return", "Show me your affection", "I will wait for you" and "Rico cafecito".

"Amor del mar" and "La leyenda de tus ojos" were recorded by Billo's Caracas Boys Orchestra, in the voice of Rafa Galindo.[xxiii]

Ricardo Mora is the artistic name of the composer, guitarist, violinist, bugle player and acoustic guitar luthier *Ricardo Mora Torres*, who was born in Puriscal in 1915 or 1920, according to the source consulted, and died in March 1994.

He was known as *"Reca"* Mora

He wrote about 140 songs and was the introducer in the popular music of that country of the rhythms of the Guarí and the Garabito, of his own inspiration.

At the age of 19 he published his first song **"¿Por qué me engañas, corazón?"** a bolero broadcast internationally by the **Trio Cantarrecio**, from Mexico, which was followed, among others: **"Después fuiste tú"**, **"Carmen"**, **"Ya no quiero que vuelvas"**, **"Para mi madre"** and **"Noche inolvidable"**, performed by the child **Eduardo Blanco**, and its recording was made on the radio station Radio para ti. It was a 45 r.p.m. single on whose B-side he placed **"Why are you deceiving me, heart?"**.

"**Unforgettable Night**" would later be performed by **Sadia Silou** (from Brazil), the **Caravelli Orchestra** (from France), **La Sonora Santanera** (from Mexico), **"Rafa" Pérez and Gilberto Hernández** (both from Costa Rica), and **Julio Jaramillo** (from Ecuador), among others.[xxiv]

Jorge Duarte was a bolero singer, who was born in San José on February 24, 1922 and died in the same city on October 4, 2010.

For many years he was one of the main voices of the **Lubín Barahona Orchestra** and the **Caballeros del Ritmo**, with which he performed in Colombia, Panama and the United States.

During his long career he recorded several albums as a soloist, of which "Jorge Duarte ayer, hoy y siempre" stand out; "Éxitos de Jorge Duarte" and "Jorge Duarte: Melodías de siempre".

Two of the boleros he performed identified him: "**Noche azul**" and "**Donde tu estás**."xxv

The 8 great Costa Rican boleros

On September 24, 2017, the Web announced the title of the eight great boleros of Costa Rica, in the opinion of the cultural manager of Guanacaste Beatriz Vargas, and the cultural heritage preserver Ligia Torijano,
Are:
"**Eso es imposible**", of Ray Tico.
"**Noche inolvidable**", of Ricardo Mora.
"**Luna liberiana**", of Jesús Bonilla Chavarría
"**Recordando mi puerto**", of Orlando Zeledón.
"**Cartaginesa**", of Carlos María Hidalgo.
"**Déjame soñar**", of Paco Navarrete.
"**Comprometido**".
"**Nada**", of Hugo Castillo.
However, there are other boleros that have enjoyed popularity, such as "**Recuérdame**" by Ricardo Mora, "**Dialoguemos**", "**Me quedo callado**" and others by Ray Tico, "**Sol de mi tierra**" by Heriberto Apú Vallejos and

"**Ciudad perdida**" by Los 8 grandes boleros costarricenses.[xxvi]

ECUADOR

This country contributed to the history of bolero great emblematic figures, both in composition and in interpretation.

Julio Jaramillo, artistic name of *Julio Alfredo Jaramillo Laurido*, was its greatest exponent in the second line. He was known as *"**The Nightingale of America**"* and was born in Guayaquil on October 1, 1935 and died in the same city on February 9, 1942.

He recorded his productions with Discos Onix, Sonolux, Discos Peerless, Codiscos, Discos Tropical (Discos Fuentes), Discomoda, VeneVox (Fonográfica Gilmar) and Yoyo Music.

In addition to bolero, he performed pasillo and waltz.

At the age of 16 he won a radio contest whose prize was his presentation in a nightclub and this fact marked the beginning of his professional career.

He lived for many years in Venezuela.

His main record productions were Ritmos venezolanos with the Trio Caracas, Sacrificio, Ojos que matan, Los Éxitos del Inmortal and 18 boleros.

He popularized, among many others, the songs **"Nuestro Juramento"**, **"Dos Años"**, **"Un disco más"**, **"Azabache"**, **"Niégalo Todo"**, **"Arrepentida"** and **"Rondando tu esquina"**.

Olimpo Cárdenas, stage name of singer Olimpo *León Cárdenas Moreira*, who was born in Vinces on July 5, 1922 and died in Tuluá, Colombia, on July 28, 1981.

He was known as *"**The King of Style**"*.

His professional life began in 1941 and ended in 1981.

At the age of 10 she sang in children's programs of La Voz del Litoral.

He shared stages in Colombia, the United States, Canada, Guatemala, Honduras, El Salvador, Venezuela, Panama, Puerto Rico and the Dominican Republic, among others, and Mexico, where he recorded 20 full-length albums.

Among many of the popular songs are **"Lágrimas de amor"**, **"Temeridad"**, **"Playita mía"**, **"Tu duda y la mía"**, **"Fatalidad"**, **"Cinco centavitos"** and **"Licor bendito"**.

Segundo Bautista was a musician, composer, pianist and guitarist who was born in Salcedo, Cotopaxi, on December 23, 1933 and died in Quito on May 8, 2019.

He composed more than 300 songs from boleros to Inca fox.

His best-known work was **"Necklace of Tears"**.

His songs were interpreted, in addition to Ecuadorian artists, by the trios "Los Tres Caballeros", "Los Panchos" and "Los Tres Diamantes".

He founded the trio "Luz de América".

Lucho Bowen was the stage name of singer *Luis Enrique Bowen Gómez* who was born in Guayaquil on August 11, 1926 and died in Cali, Colombia, on April 30, 2005.

Many of his hits were recorded with the RCA Victor and Fuentes labels.

His repertoire was made up, among many other songs, of **"Amor de copas"**, **"Mi castigo"**, **"Inútilmente"**, **"En ese más allá"**, **"Nuestros corazones"**, **"Esperando tu amor"**, **"Granitos de arena"**, **"Se me olvidó tu** nombre", "Cría cuervos", "Verdad amarga", "A veces los recuerdos", "You're going to cry for me", "Loving is sin", "Don't cry heart", "I'm moving away from you", "Leave me in peace", "I'll love you in silence", "Crying your departure", "I want to save you", "Yolanda", "Tears of love" and "Cry heart".

Julio César Villafuerte a musician, composer, singer and arranger who was born in Jipijapa, Manabí, on January 1, 1928, and adopted Colombian nationality in March 2007.

He composed pasacalle, pasillo, bolero, ranchera and Peruvian waltz.

From 1951 to 1959 he formed a duet with **Lucho Bowen.**

Julio Jaramillo and **Olimpo Cárdenas** were interpreters of some of his songs, such as "**Arrepentida**" and "**Tu Duda y la Mía**".

He has also written the songs "**Corazón prisionero**", "**La pena de no verte**", "**Mi Jipijapa querido**", "**Vida de mi vida**", "**De cigarro en cigarro**", "**Amor de una madre**", "**Sueña, sueña muchachita**", "**Sin rumbo**", "**Alma Lojana**", "**Primorosa**", "**Ausente Madre Mía**", "**Between Tavern and Tavern**".[xxvii]

BOLIVIA

In this country, the bolero is expressed passively, through shows enlivened by foreign artists, and actively with vernacular performers and composers.

Raúl Shaw Moreno was the artistic name with which the composer and performer *Raúl Shaw Boutier* became known, who was born in Oruro on November 30, 1923 and died in Buenos Aires, Argentina, on April 13, 2003.

He belonged to the trio "Los Panchos".

In 1946 with his brother Víctor Shaw, he founded the trio "Los Altiplánicos", which allowed him to become known in his country.

Two years later he formed the trio "Los Indios" with which he performed in Mexico,

Later, together with the Valdez brothers, he was part of the trio "Panamérica Antawara", with which he made his first recording. Around that time, he wrote his first hit, the bolero "**Magaly**".

Together with "Los Panchos" he performed on the most important stages throughout Latin America, including successful presentations in Brazil and also in Japan.

With this group he recorded, among others, the boleros "**Esos Ojos verdes**", "**Quiéreme mucho**", "**Perfidia**", "**Bésame Mucho**", "**Solamente Una vez**", "**María Elena**", "**Amigos**" and "**Lágrimas de Amor**", of his authorship.

Later, in the company of Fernando Rossi and José González, he formed the trio "Los Peregrinos", making his debut on Radio Corporación de Santiago and performing his first songs, such as "**Cuando tú me quieras**" and "**Lágrimas de Amor**".

He was also the author of the boleros "**Sólo cenizas**", "**Que saben de mí**" and "**El Espejo**".[xxviii]

Los Genios is a trio created on October 15, 1965. On the occasion of the group's half-century, Jorge Soruco wrote the following report in the newspaper *La Razón*:

On October 18, 1965, three teenagers between the ages of 16 and 18 decided to form a trio. They did not imagine that 50 years later the music of Los Genios would continue to summon the Bolivian public to their concerts.

"We were very young and adventurous boys. When we decided to form the group, we were between 16 and 18 years old, and we did not expect it to become our way of life,"

recalls Víctor Córdoba, the composer, guitarist and founder of the La Paz trio.

However, despite its youth, the group quickly became one of the most successful of its generation, with more than a hundred albums published and tours of the country and abroad.

To celebrate their golden anniversary, Los Genios prepared a year full of special activities, which will begin on the 14th and 15th of this month with the performance of their traditional Concert for the Mother at the Alberto Saavedra Pérez Municipal Theater at 7:00 p.m. (Genaro Sanjinés Street).

The story of Los Genios also has to do with the formation of a family. Sometime after the trio was formed, the composer and guitarist Víctor Córdoba and Alcira Arteaga, the singer, married and became the nucleus of the group. *"More than a group we are a family, since now it is our son Xavier who accompanies us as his brother José Luis did before,"* says the voice.

This solidity allowed them to remain one of the most prolific groups in Bolivia, with at least two hundred albums published on different labels. With Discolandia alone they produced 50 albums and on their walls they exhibit six gold records, two double platinum and three triple platinum records by Lauro.

This trajectory also made it possible for their careers to expand. For example, Víctor composed for various groups and institutions; Some of these songs will be presented at the week's concerts.

They also founded their own record company, Córdoba Producciones, although they experienced a major setback: 15 years ago they were victims of a robbery and only in recent years began to recover.

This is how, in the second half of this year, just for the anniversary, they will release a compilation album with songs from their different stages, including those they dedicated to mothers, such as "**Madre de los cabellos de plata**", the bolero "**Lo que quiso el destino**", national songs such as "**El durazno**" and "**Matecito de toronjil**" and even the songs they composed for soccer teams such as "**At four in the afternoon**," for Bolívar.

The success is attributed to a combination of an eclectic repertoire and to the fact that *"we were able to escape the process of standardization of Bolivian folk music that emerged after Los Kjarkas,"* says Xavier Córdova.

And now the founders are seeing their legacy come to life in their grandchildren, some of whom are already singing. *"It's nice to see that it is confirmed that what is inherited is not stolen and that there will be Los Genios for a long time,"* says Alcira.

BRASIL

In this country, the bolero has many representatives, both in the area of interpretation and composition.

Altemar Dutra, stage name of *Altemar Dutra de Oliveira*, called "***The King of Brazilian Bolero***" and born in Minas Garais on October 6, 1940, and died while performing in New York on November 9, 1983.

In 1980 he recorded Siempre Romántico - 25 Boleros Inolvidables

His main hits were "**Peleas**", "**Vete de mí**", "**He sabido que te amaba**" and "**¿Qué quieres tú de mí?**".

She began her career acting for the Radio Difusora de Colatina, in Espírito Santo – a town where her family had moved.

He recorded his first album on the Tiger label with the title: Saudade que vem (Magalhães and Célio Ferreira) and Somente uma vez (Luís Mergulhão e Roberto Moreira).

We read about him in Wikipedia, the free encyclopedia:
-Around 1963, he was taken by Amorim to the program Boleros Dentro da Noite of Radio Mundial, the same year Joãozinho of the Yrakitan Trio, presented him in Odeon where he signed a contract, he managed to place himself at the top of the popularity lists with the song Tudo de mim (Evaldo Gouveia and Jair Amorim) achieving the well-known throughout Brazil.

He recorded an LP together with **Lucho Gatica**.

Miltinho, whose real name is *Milton Santos de Almeida*, born in Rio de Janeiro on January 31, 1929 and died in the same city on November 8, 2014. He popularized the pieces, "**Dedo de guante**", "**Cuando estamos viejos**",

"**Pecadora**", "**Amor de pobre**", and "**Quien yo quiero no me quiere**", among others.

He was called "*The King of Phrasing*".

His extensive discography, in Portuguese and Spanish, included, among many others, the albums Billo-Miltiño-Doctores en Ritmo (1959) with **Billo Frómeta**, Miltinho (1961), Os Grandes Sucessos de Miltinho (1963), Dulce Veneno (1964), Su Estilo Y Su Canciones (1966), Amor de Pobre (1967), Tu Imagen (1967), Canta En Castellano (1968). El Rey Del Fraseo (1969) and Hablemos de Amor Otra Vez (1969).

Roberto Carlos, stage name *Roberto Carlos Braga Moreira*, singer-songwriter born in Cachoeiro de Itapemirim, on April 19, 1941.

He has sold more than 150 million records in various parts of the world.

Grammy winner.

He was for many years the only Latin American singer to win the Song Festival in San Remo.

She sang in English, Portuguese and Spanish.

In 1981 he toured internationally and recorded his first album in English; the others would be in Spanish, Italian and French. He also recorded the annual album, which included hits such as "**Emociones**", "**Cama y Mesa**" and "**Ballenas**"

In 1992 he engraved his name on the Miami Walk of Fame (United States) for Latin American artists.

Simone, whose real name is *Simone Bittencourt de Oliveira*, born in Bahia on December 26, 1949, interpreter of "**La hiedra**", "**Quiero amanecer con alguien** " and "**Mi amor**", among others.

She has sung both in her mother tongue, Portuguese, and in Spanish, obtaining a success similar to that of her compatriot **Roberto Carlos**, also being recognized in the Spanish-speaking world.

In 1976 she recorded the song "**O**" which will be the theme of the novel Doña Flor and her two husbands.

In 1978 she released Cigarra, her fifth LP, which includes the song of the same name composed especially for her by **Milton Nascimento**. His discography is extensive, and among his best-known and reissued songs are "**Procuro olvidarte**" (by the Spanish composer Manuel Alejandro), "**Popurrí**" (with songs belonging to the Mexican singer and composer Armando Manzanero) and others by his compatriot **Roberto Carlos**. She has also sung a duet with the Cuban **Pablo Milanés**.

Nelson Ned, artistic name of *Nelson Ned D'Ávila Pinto*, born in Ubá on March 2, 1947 and died in Cotia, on January 5, 2014, called "**The Little Giant of Song**". He was also an author. He recorded in Spanish the albums "**Si Las Flores Pudo Hablar**", "**Nelson en Acción**", "**Jesús está vivo**", "**Jesús te ama**", "**Jesús es vida**" and "**Mi testimonio**".

Chico Buarque, *He* was born in Rio de Janeiro on June 19, 1944. He is also a singer of boleros and other genres, a guitarist, novelist, poet and playwright.

He popularized the songs "**Que será**", "**Mar y Luna**", "**A pesar de usted**", "**Querido amigo**", "**Constructor**", "**Te amo**" and "**Cotidiano**", among many others.

His public debut as a musician and composer – according to Wikipedia, the free encyclopedia – occurred in 1964 and he soon made a name for himself through his participation in music festivals and television programs.

His discography is extensive, and he recorded with the RGE and Philips labels.

Lindomar Castilho, stage name of singer and musician *Lindomar Cabral*, who was born in Santa Helena de Goiás on January 21, 1940 and died on March 30, 1981.

He popularized the boleros "**Você é doida demais**" (You are crazy too much) and "**Eu amo a sua mãe**" (I love his mother).

He sang bolero and soul.

He was one of the biggest record sellers in the 1970s and his productions were released simultaneously in the United States and Brazil.

His style influenced a whole generation of singers.

Los Indios Tabajaras. *Mussapere and Herundy*, both brothers, were born in the deep jungle of the state of Ceará, in northeastern Brazil, then they were renamed Antenor and Natalicio Moreyra Lima, under the epithet of Los Indios Tabajaras.

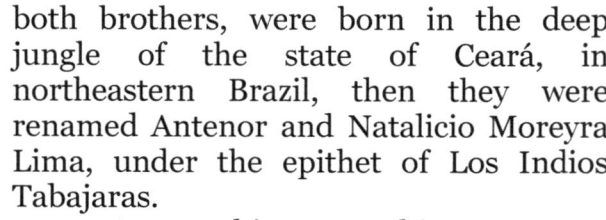

Among his many hit songs are "**Frenesí, Martha**", "**Tema del Tercer Hombre**", "**Amapola**", "**El Pájaro Campana**", "**El Cóndor Pasa**", "**Recuerdos de la Alhambra**", "**María**

Elena", "Begin The Beguine", "No Tengo Lágrimas", "Cuando Vuelve a Tu Lado", "El Mar", " Mamá Yo Quiero", "Valse en C-Sharp", "Lamento Borincano", "El Amor Es Una Cosa Esplendorosa", "Johnny Guitar", and "Humo en Tus Ojos", among many more.

Agostinho dos Santos, was a bolero and bossa singer and composer who was born in Sao Paulo on April 25, 1932 and died in Orly, France, on July 11, 1973. Among his hits in Spanish are the songs "**Tu Y Yo**", "**Tonada Triste**", "**La noche de mi amor**", "**Escríbeme**", "**Noche sin fin**", "**Ahora**", "**Lourdes**", "**Una vez más**", "**Esmeralda**", "**Horóscopo**", "**Perfidia**", "**Angustia**", "**Noche de ronda**", "**Esos ojos verdes**", "**Gracias**" and "**Orfeo Negro**".

Nana Caymmi is the stage name of the singer *Dinair Tostes Caymmi*, born in Rio de Janeiro on April 29, 1941.

In 1961 she participated in a contest singing the song "**Acalanto**" and shortly after she moved with her husband to Venezuela, spending some years away from the artistic environment.

Back in Brazil, she released her first album, "Nana". In 1966, he participated in the I International Song Festival, winning first place with the song "**Saveiros**".

She is considered one of the most expressive and refined interpreters of Brazilian music, celebrated for the sophistication of both her interpretations of popular songs and songs composed especially for her.

In 2003 he recorded for the public the album Boleros, containing a selection of 14 classic boleros, of which 13 are sung in Spanish.

Orquesta Serenata Tropical, of which we read in "El Blog del Bolero" that its reputation was such that, in Wikipedia, when talking about the history of the bolero and identifying its interpreters by countries, it is alluded to that in Brazil among the great promoters of that noble and romantic rhythm are the "Tropical Serenade Orchestra" and the orchestra "Los Románticos de Cuba".

According to that source. Its origins date back to the early 60s and it was active until 2004.

He recorded several volumes entitled "Solamente Boleros". That instrumental musical group performed, among many others, the songs "**Obsession**", "**Nostalgia Habanera**", "**Mil gracias**", "**Muñeca de cera**", "**Voy**", "**Si no eres tú**", "**Lamento gitano**", "**Bajo un palmar**", "**Celos de ti**", "**Amor perdido**", "**Sin ti**", "**Tres words**", "**Our oath**", "**Those green eyes**", "**A whole life**", "**The boat**", "**Perfidia**" and "**You got me used to** it".

Románticos de Cuba was an orchestra created within the Musidisc label by its owner, **Nilo Sérgio**.

Its period of activity lasted from 1959 to 1981.

Period in activity   1959 – 1981.

Among his hits are "**Bésame mucho**", "**Quiéreme mucho**", "**Vereda tropical**", "**Perdón**", "**Usted**", "**Gema**", "**No me quieres tanto**", "**Cerca del mar**", "**La gloria eres tú**" and "**Noche de ronda**".[xxix]

COLOMBIA

This South American country made great asides in the history of the bolero, both in interpretation, composition and innovation.

He contributed the bolero Vallenato.

According to Jesús Rincón Murcia, in a digital text of June 4, 1991, the most outstanding Colombian bolero singers, in his opinion, were Jorge Añez, who is said to have composed the first, (Te amo); Jaime R. Echavarría (Me estás haciendo falta); Lucho Bermúdez (Añoranzas); Álvaro Dalmar (Proud); Rafael Mejía (As long as you love me); Santander Díaz (I fell in love with you); José Barros (Busco tu recuerdo); Faustino Arias (Noches de Bocagrande); Oscar Fajardo (Lost and Loveless); Eduardo Arias (Rafael Roncallo (Corazón), among others. Obviously, some of them have more production.

Charlie Zaa, stage name of *Carlos Alberto Sánchez Ramírez*, who was born in Girardot on July 22, 1971. He has a tenor voice.

His discography is integrated, among others, by the albums Sentimientos, Un segundo sentimiento, The Remixes, Ciego de amor, De un solo sentimiento, Grandes sentimientos and Puro sentimiento.

He innovated the bolero in his country by updating famous songs by **Julio Jaramillo**.

Faustino Arias, stage name of *Faustino Arias Reynel*, poet and composer born on April 13, 1910 in Barbacoas, Nariño, and died in Tumaco on July 29, 1985 in Tumaco, also in Nariño.

He set to music the beautiful piece "**Alma tumaqueña**" written by the doctor and also poet from Tumaco Manuel Benítez Duclerq.

He is also the author of the songs "**Sueño tropical**", "**Rosario de besos**", "**Porteña**", "**Aguabajo**", "**Mi pueblo**", "**Sindamanoy**" and the controversial song "**Noches de Bocagrande**" whose dedication was disputed by the city of Cartagena, being really addressed to the Island of Bocagrande in Tumaco. He was married to Lola González Hincapié, a lady from Filandia, Quindío, who until recently was based in the city of Cali. This marriage produced seven children: Isabella, Faustino, Oscar, Eduardo, Fernando, Roberto and Lilú. Several institutions or dependencies in Nariño bear the name of this great man who died at the age of 75. Unquestionable pride of Nariño.

José Barros, By the stage name of *José Benito Barros Palomino*, he was the most prolific Colombian composer of popular music. He composed Fecundo paseos, cumbias, porros, pasillos, boleros, tangos, currulaos, merengues, etc.

He was born in El Banco, Magdalena, on March 21, 1915 and died in Santa Marta on May 12, 2007.

His best-known bolero, "**Busco tu recuerdo**", was performed by the most well-known bolero singers, such as **Daniel Santos**.

Santander Díaz, Carlos *Arturo Díaz Herrera* was born in San Juan Nepomuceno Bolívar on May 11, 1933 and died in Bogotá on September 15, 1990.

He was a member of the famous bolero trio "Los Isleños".

One of her songs, "**La sombra**", reached the entire Spanish-speaking world in the voice of Claudia from Colombia.

"**Me enamoré de ti**" is another of his famous boleros,

With that group he visited the United States and South America.

Rafael Mejía, artistic name of *Rafael David Mejía Romani*, considered by many specialists as the most important romantic composer in Colombia, despite having started with the bambuco and the pasillo. He was born in Barranquilla on March 27, 1920, and died in his hometown on July 18, 2003.

He produced approximately 150 songs.

His bolero "**Mientras me quieres tú**", performed by **Leo Marini**, catapulted him as one of the most important cultists of this genre in Colombia. Also his are the boleros "**Vidas iguales**", "**Nadie más que tú**", "**Por Dios que eres bonita**", "**Despierta corazón**", "**Ahí estás tú**", "**Sabes muy bien**", "**Más y más**" and "**Será por eso**". His work is completed with merengues, rancheras, porros, bagpipes and guarachas.

Lucho Bermúdez, stage name of *Luis Eduardo Bermúdez Acosta*, musician, composer, arranger, director and performer of Colombian popular music, born in Carmen

de Bolívar on January 25, 1912 and died in Bogotá on April 23, 1994.

He wrote bagpipes, boleros, mapalé, cumbia, fandango and porro, etc.

Among his boleros is **"Nostalgias"**.

He recorded about 80 albums and composed about a thousand songs.

Jaime R. Echavarría, stage name of *Jaime Rudesindo Echavarría Villegas*, singer-songwriter and politician born in Medellín on November 13, 1923, and died in the same city on January 29, 2010.

Among his hits are "**Me estás haciendo falta**", "**Cuando voy por la calle**", "**Yo nací para ti**", "**Qué tienes tú**", "**Serenata de amor**", "**María Inés**", "**Entre estas cuatro paredes**", "**Llévame de la mano**", "**Adorada**" and "**Sueño**", among others.

Jorge Añez was a singer and composer, born in Bogotá in April 1892 and died in the same city on July 22, 1953.

Among his songs are "**Los cucaracheros**", "**Agáchate el sombrerito**", "**Ausencia**", "**Óyeme bien mío**" and "**Te amo**", considered the first Colombian bolero.

In 1950 he wrote one of the first books on Colombian popular song, "**Songs and Memories**".

He was part of the groups Lira Colombiana, the Trío Colombiano, the Estudiantina Áñez and the duet Briceño y Añez.

Carlos Julio Ramírez, who was born in Tocaima, Cundinamarca, on August 4, 1916, and died in Miami, United States, on December 12, 1986. He was a lyrical and popular music singer.

His bolero repertoire was made up, among others, of the songs "**Mala noche**", "**Romanza de amor**", "**Nostalgias**", "**Perfidia**", "**Frenesí**", "**Mi canción**", "**Dame de tu rosa**", "**Granada**", "**Dime que sí**", "**Júrame**", "**Así**", "**Mis flores negras**" and "**Why remember**".

Nelson Pinedo, stage name of *Napoleón Nelson Pinedo Fedullo*, singer and composer, who was born in Barranquilla on February 10, 1928, and died in Valencia, Venezuela, on October 27, 2016.

He was called "*The Admiral of Rhythm*" and "*El Pollo Barranquillero*".

He acted as vocalists of La Sonora Matancera, where among other hits he performed the boleros, "**Señora Bonita**", "**Desesperación**", "**Corazón sin Puerto**", and "**Quién será**".

He recorded for RCA Víctor de México and Discomoda, from Caracas.

Álvaro Dalmar, stage name of *Álvaro Chaparro Bermúdez*, composer and singer, who was born in Bogotá on March 7, 1917 and died in the same city on May 18, 1999. His first composition was the bambuco "**El Diablito**", which he later recorded by Manuel Astudillo in New York.

In the 50s he composed songs especially for **Carlos Julio Ramírez**, which were successful in Colombia such as "**Bésame, morenita**" was his most representative song. At the same time, he composed songs for the Venezuelan singer

Alfredo Sadel, including "**Un beso de amor**", "**Lindo soy yo**", "**Lágrimas**" and "**Todito el año**". At the same time his boleros made history with the Dalmar Trio.

In addition to the singers already mentioned, their compositions were also heard in the voices of the Venezuelan **Felipe Pirela**, Venezuelan, who popularized the bolero "**Amor se escribe con llanto**", Los Hermanos Martínez, "**Angustias**", "**Di que no me quieres**" and "**Me desperté sin ti**"; Orquesta Aragón, "**Cosas cositas**" and María América Samudio, "**Padrenuestro**", "**Ave María**" and "**Feliz Cumpleaños**".

Oscar Fajardo is the stage name of *Oscar Fajardo García*, creator of the famous trio "Los Isleños", a bastion of  bolero in Colombia. He was born in Ocaña, Norte de Santander, on an unspecified date in 1927, and died in Bogotá on September 24, 2000, according to Caracol Radio. He was 73 years old.

He was the author of the boleros "**Perdido y sin amor**" and "**Sangre en el río**", among many others.

Twenty boleros with all the Colombian flavor was the title given by the editorial staff of the newspaper *El Tiempo* on May 15, 1993 to the publication of the two-disc album by the singer María Cristina De la Espriella constant of the songs "**Cuando te vuelve a ver**", "**Cartagena contigo**", "**Me enamoré de ti**", "**I look for you**", "**Desirous**", "**If I kiss you again, I wish**", "**As long as you love me**", "**Bocagrande nights**", "**So far away**", "**You're missing me**", "**Taganga**", "**My reality**", "**I love you**", "**I'm alone**", "**What is love**", "**A la orilla del mar**", "**Perdida sin** amor", "**Corazón**" and " **Si vuelvo a enamorarme**", by the Colombian composers Leonor Campo de Lega, Alfonso De la Espriella, Santander Díaz, Lucho Bermúdez, Eduardo Cabas, Jaime Llano González, Darío Corredor, Rafael Mejía, Faustino Arias, Álvaro Dalmar, Jaime R. Echavarría, Nacho Dugand, Jorge Añez, Graciela Arango de Tobón, José Barros, Oscar Fajardo, Rafael Roncallo and Mario Gareña.

Claudia de Colombia, is the stage name of the singer *Blanca Gladys Caldas Méndez*, born in Bogotá on January 18, 1950.

She has performed on stages in his country, Venezuela, Argentina, Ecuador, Puerto Rico, Miami, Panama, Dominican Republic, Costa Rica, Uruguay, Mexico, he also sounded in Spain, Brazil, Paraguay and Suriname.

Among the hits performed are, among many others, "**Amor se escribe con llano**", "**Tú me haces falta**", "**Hoy daba yo la vida**", "**La sombra**", "**Nuestra historia de amor**", "**Tú me acostumbraste**", "**Quisiera tener te a pesar de todo**", "**Vivo enamorada**", "**La vida es un sueño**", "**Ay destino ay mi amigo**", "**El ocaso de un amor**" and "**Surprised**".

Tito Cortez was the stage name of *José Alberto Cortés Bonnet* "***El Ciclón Colombiano***" who went "to sing to heaven" and make a duet in the celestial choirs, with his friend and colleague Piper Pimienta, as El Tiempo pointed out when reviewing his death, two days after it occurred. He was born in Tumaco, Nariño, on an unspecified date of 1929? and died in Cali on July 18, 1998. He sang and composed boleros. He was the author of

110 albums, including **"El Diablo"**, **"Reconciliación"**, **"Si te vas"**, **"Mala Mujer"**, **"Alma Tumaqueña"**.[xxx]

REPÚBLICA DOMINICANA.

Many names have bequeathed this country to the history of bolero both in composition and in interpretation.

Alberto Beltrán, the stage name of the singer *Alberto Amancio Beltrán* was known for the merengue "**El negrito del Batey**", but also for his boleros "**Although it costs me life**", "**I ignore your existence**", "**El 19**" and "**Todo me gusta de ti**".

He was born in the town of Palo Blanco, in the province of La Romana, on May 5, 1923, and died in Miami, United States, on February 2, 1997.

"From 1946 to 1951," reads Wikipedia, the free encyclopedia, "he belonged to several groups in his country, such as "Brisas de Oriente." Later, he formed his own group called "Dominican Boys".

The same source reveals that *"In 1951 he emigrated to Puerto Rico"* and *"There, he recorded with "Los Diablos del Caribe", Mario Hernández's group, the song "El 19".* Later, *"he traveled to Cuba, first to Santiago and then to Havana on July 15, 1954, to work with the Puerto Rican composer and singer Myrta Silva on Radio Mambí,"* with whom he was until *"August 16 of that same year,"* when *"he was required by the Sonora Matancera and recorded the composition Ignoro tu existencia by Rafael Pablo de la Motta and Although it costs me the life of the inspiration of the Dominican Luis Kalaff. Both songs, to the rhythm of bolero, were recorded on the same 78 r.p.m. disc."*.

He was with that group until *"El 18 de enero de 1955"*. He immediately went to Venezuela and left phonographic recordings with the orchestras "Sonora Caracas", Los

Megatones de Lucho and the Orchestra of **Jesús "Chucho" Sanoja**, Likewise, "Hired by the Dominican musician settled in Venezuela, **Billo Frómeta**, he participated in two albums recorded in studios in Cuba: "Evocación" (1956) in which he performed as a soloist and "La Lisa-Maracaibo", in which he shared credits with Cuban singer Carlos Díaz."

Rafael Bullumba Landestoy, is the stage name of the composer and pianist *Pedro Rafael "Peter" Landestoy Duluc*, born in La Romana on August 18, 1924, and died in Santo Domingo on July 17, 2018.

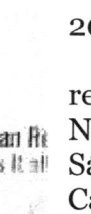

It was active from 1950 to 2007.

His bolero "**Pesar**" was recorded by Daniel Santos, Toña la Negra, Panchito Riset, Alcibiades Sánchez with the orchestra Billo's Caracas Boys, the Janitzio Trio, Alberto Beltrán and Miltinho.

In Mexico, the artist Fernando Fernández made his songs "**Carita de ángel**" and "**Mi dulce querer" into films**. Similarly, the interpreter Lupita Palomera recorded her bolero "**Sin necesidad** ", Toña la Negra and Milagros Lanty recorded the song "**Yo soy mulata**" and Juan Arvizu recorded the bolero "**Incomprensión**".

He lived in Venezuela and Mexico during the dictatorship of Rafael Leónidas Trujillo and at the end of 1950 he moved to New York where he performed as a pianist in different musical groups.

He had a vast and profound musical work and was the luckiest Dominican composer internationally.

Papá Molina is the stage name of the musician, director and composer *Ramón Antonio Molina*, born in Moca, on December 19, 1925. On September 29, 2011, the National

Council of Culture of his country declared him "**National Glory of Dominican Music**", in recognition of his musical work and the role played in the projection of popular music.

His most popular bolero "**Evocación**" was recorded, among others, by Alci Sánchez, Alberto Beltrán and the orchestra of Billo Frómeta, Rafael Colón and Betty Misiego.

He also wrote "**Sufro por ti**", performed by Alberto Beltrán and the San José Super Orchestra; "**I've never told you**", in the voice of Lope Balaguer; and "**Cuando volveré a besarte**", with versions by Elenita Santos and Rafael Colón.

Mario de Jesús, stage name of composer and music editor *Mario César de Jesús Báez*, who was born in San Pedro de Macoris and died in Mexico on July 20, 2008.

He is considered the most prolific composer of boleros in his country, and his compositions were performed, among others, by Marco Antonio Muñiz, María Luisa Landín, Trio Los Panchos, Lucía Méndez, Lucho Gatica, La Sonora Matancera, Pérez Prado, Libertad Lamarque, Plácido Domingo and Luis Miguel.

In 1952 the Cuban Bienvenido Granda accompanied by the Sonora Matancera recorded the bolero "**No toques ese disco**", his first success as a composer.

He settled in Mexico in 1959, in whose capital he founded in March 1968 the Latin American Musical Publisher (EMLASA) and in 1975 he inaugurated Leo Musical.

"**¿Y qué hiciste del amor que me brindaste?**", "**Adelante**", "**Ayúdame Dios mío**", "**Que se mueran de envidia**", "**Cría cuervos**", "**Perdámonos**", "**Ya la**

pagarás", "**Cumbia del torero**" y "**O...**", entre otras, dieron de comer a Libertad Lamarque, Luis Miguel, Los Panchos, Vicente Fernández, Julio Iglesias, Vicky Car, Lucía Méndez, María Luisa Landin, Lucho Gatica, La Sonora Matancera y Pérez Prado, entre muchos otros.

With an extremely intense life in the recording field, Mario de Jesús founded the Editora Mexicana de Música Internacional in Mexico City, after becoming independent from major record labels.

Héctor Acosta is *Héctor Elpidio Acosta Restituyo*, known as "*El Tonto*", a merengue, bachata and bolero singer and composer and producer.

He was born on May 23, 1967, in Bonao.

Among her hits are, among others, the songs "**Mi niña**", "**Primavera azul**", "**Lo que tiene ella**", "**Perdóname la vida**" and "**Me duele la cabeza**".

He has taken his music to much of Latin America, the United States, Spain, Switzerland and Italy.

Jackeline Estévez is the stage name of *Rumualda Jackeline Estévez Rodríguez*, born on February 7, 1968 in San Francisco de Macorís, Duarte, and singer of bolero, ballad and pop.

He began his career in 1982, in the program Fiesta de Teleantillas, achieving great popularity, sharing the stage with prominent international figures such as: José José, Alfredo Sadel, Leo Marini, Álvaro Torres, Nelson Ned and Camilo Sesto, among others.

Her discography until 2010 was as follows: "Crisálida", "Demuéstremelo" and "Lléname de besos", 1983, "Toda tuya", 1994, "Jackeline Estévez, sus 18 más grandes éxitos", 2005, "Mujer Enamorada", 2007, and "Única en boleros".

Also, the singles "**Crisálida**", "**Yo soy**", "**Ese día llegará**" and "**Hoy por qué no te has gone**".

Francis Santana is the stage name of *Juan Francisco Santana*, born in the Dominican capital and died in the same city on January 11, 2014.

It was active from 1943 to 2008.

He was known as "*El Songo*".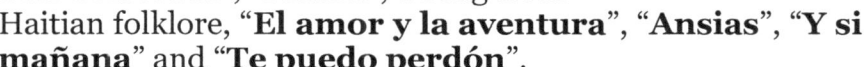

He was a bolero and son singer.

Some of the compositions that became popular in his voice were "**Salve San Cristóbal**", "**Massá**", a song from Haitian folklore, "**El amor y la aventura**", "**Ansias**", "**Y si mañana**" and "**Te puedo perdón**".

His discography included the recordings: "100 canciones y un millón de recuerdos" (1970), "El Papaupa!", "La salsa de Santo Domingo" (1971), "Francis Santana" (1976), "En son de felicidad" (1977), "Entre tú y yo" (1978), "Sancocho" (1980), "El Disco de Oro" (2000), "Reserva Musical" (2006) and "¡Esto Es Bolero!" (2010).

Luis Kalaff was a prolific composer, guitarist and performer who was born in Santo Domingo on October 11, 1916, and died in the same city on July 2, 2010.

He built his first guitar himself, at the age of fourteen.

He bequeathed to popular musical history two immortal boleros, "**Although I Cost the Diva**" and "**Love Without Hope**".

This artist took mangulina to the radio and composed almost two thousand songs.

He has also authored the boleros "**Acuérdate de mí**", "**El que me robó tu amor**" and "**Estoy a tu orden**". He also composed the merengues "**La empalizá**", "**La tuerca**", "**Cuando yo me muera**", "**La mina**" and "**El colorao**".

It should be noted that bachata originates from the Dominican Republic, considered a derivation of the rhythmic bolero, with influences from other styles such as Cuban son and merengue.

Lope Balaguer was the stage name of the singer *José Manuel López Balaguer*, who was born in Santiago de los Caballeros on August 22, 1925, and ceased to exist in Santo Domingo on January 29, 2015. He was one of the icons of Dominican bolero interpretation.

She debuted in 1940 as a singer on the radio. He performed in Puerto Rico, Venezuela, Colombia, Guatemala, El Salvador, Panama, Haiti, Guadeloupe, Martinique and the United States.

Their discography includes the recordings of the albums Concierto de Amor (1946), Confesión de Amor (1950), Recuento (1950), Lope Balaguer y la Orquesta San José (1960), Serrana (1960), Habrá Un Nuevo Mundo Por Amor (1968), El Lope Balaguer de Hoy y de Siempre (1969), Álbum de Oro (1975), Algo Contigo y Me Siento Bien Contigo (1976), Aquellos Años Cuarenta y Espectacular. (1977), Álbum de Oro (1980), 45 Aniversario con el Arte: ¡Tradición de Calidad! (1986), Mi Vida Es Una Canción (1988), Álbum de Oro (1990), containing more than 200 titles, including: **"Noche De Amor"**, **"Concierto De Amor"**, **"Amor, Ciego"** **"Necesito De Ti"**, **"Capricho"**, **"Así es la Vida"**, **"Súplica"**, **"Adiós Vida Mía"**, **"Hoja Seca"**, **"¿Por Qué Lloras?"**, **"Sin Ti"**, **"Flor de Naranjo"**, **"Serrana"**, **"Egoísmo"**, **"Ausencia"** y **"Abrázame Así"**.[xxxi]

PANAMÁ

This country gave the history of the bolero great composers and performers.

Ricardo Fábrega was the stage name of the composer *Ricardo Fábrega*, who was born in Santiago on January 28, 1905, and died on February 10, 1973.

Author, among others, of the boleros "Taboga", "Panamá Viejo", "Cuando lejos de ti", "Bajo un palmar", "Santa Ana", "Ventana", "Madrecita", "Tu ausencia", "Por eso te quiero", "Cuando muere la tarde", "Noches de mi tierra", "Hoy vuelves a mi lado", "Por los caminos del viento", "Si tú supieras", "Riomar", "Aquella melodía", "Te vas", "Noche tropical" and "Mi lindo ranchito".

Carlos Eleta Almarán, was a composer who was born in Panama on May 16, 1918, and died in the same city on January 16, 2013.

He bequeathed to humanity the bolero **"Historia de un amor"**, written in 1956 and inspired by the death of his brother Fernando's wife.

He was also the author of "**Bolero**" and "**Lejos de ti**".[xxxii]

Arturo "Chino" Hassan was a composer, born in Panama on July 28, 1911 and died on February 9, 1974.

The bolero "**Soñar**", dedicated to his wife, became his biggest hit and with it he obtained a Gold Record in 1956.

In the same genre he also wrote the songs "Mi último bolero", "Mi ser", "Esperándote", "Morena", "Solo y triste", "Mejor así", "Esperanza negra", "Por tus ojos", "Amor o ilusión", "Mi cielo eres tú", "Estoy en tu corazón", "Tu alma",

"Cabecita loca", "Seré tu sombra", "Sin tu amor" and "La verdad", which was his last composition.

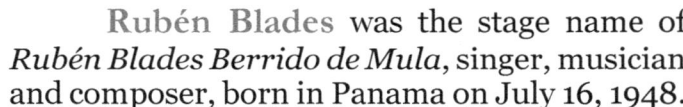

Martina Andrión, composer, called the *Alondra Coclesana*, was born in Penomé on June 9, 1907, and died in Panama City on April 13, 2005

He composed countless songs and school hymns.

Author of the boleros "**Panamá mío**", and "**Guacamaya**", from 1962, which is almost an anthem for the people of Peñanome.

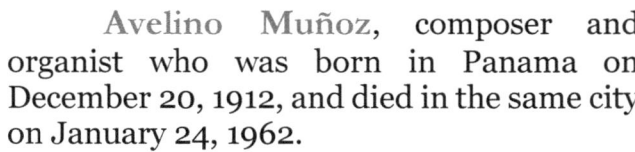

Rubén Blades was the stage name of *Rubén Blades Berrido de Mula*, singer, musician and composer, born in Panama on July 16, 1948.

He is known as an intellectual salsero, but in 1962 he recorded the boleros "**Noche de luna**", by Gonzalo Curiel and "**Vete de mí**", by Homero Expósito, on 45 rpm.

He also recorded the ticket "Hastío" from his friend Roberto Cedeño.

Avelino Muñoz, composer and organist who was born in Panama on December 20, 1912, and died in the same city on January 24, 1962.

He recorded his first album in 1938.

Among her most popular boleros are "**Eres bonita**", "**Estoy contigo**", "**Ya no me haces falta**", "**Maldición gitana**" and "**Irremediablemente solo**".[xxxiii]

NICARAGUA

This country has created tools for the cultural reproduction of the bolero and has many relevant names in the field of composition and interpretation.

Rafael Gastón Pérez, composer and musician, was born in the El Calvario neighborhood of Managua, on February 26, 1917, the most widespread date, although other versions place his birth on July 22, 1915, and assure that he was registered as *Manuel Rafael Pérez*. Trumpeter and composer. He was active from 1922 to 1962, when he died on February 4.

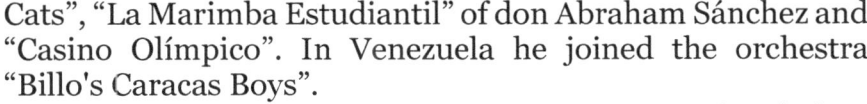

He founded the musical groups "Black Cats", "La Marimba Estudiantil" of don Abraham Sánchez and "Casino Olímpico". In Venezuela he joined the orchestra "Billo's Caracas Boys".

He performed in several countries and his bolero "**Sinceridad**" was performed, among others, by Lucho Gatica, Marco Antonio Muñiz, José Luis Rodríguez "El Puma", the pianist Raúl di Blasco, María Martha Sierra Lima, Eva Garza, Los Galos, Orlando Vallejo, the Luisito Plá trio, the Orquesta Románticos de Cuba, Bienvenido Granda with the Conjunto Casino, Roberto Yanés, The Three Diamonds, The Tecolines of Mexico, Flor de María Medina, Joao Bosco (Portuguese version that appeared in the Brazilian novel "Tieta"), Virginia López.

He also composed, among others, the boleros "**Cuando Caliente El Sol En Masachapa**", made internationally known by the Rigual Brothers as "**Cuando Caliente el sol**", "**Romance**", "**Infiel**", "**Noche De diciembre**" recorded for the first time in the voice of Felipe

Pirela with Billo's Caracas Boys. Sincerity, **"Silence of Love"** and **"María Adelina"**.

In addition, since December 2018 the National Concert of the Rafael Gastón Pérez Song Festival has been held, according to information from Nohemy Sandino It took place at the Rubén Darío National Theater in Managua.

It is also the country that is the scene of the Song Festival, from which great figures of the bolero have emerged.

In that country there is the Association of Artists of Nicaragua "Rafael Gastón Pérez", which annually awards the best Nicaraguan artists and pays permanent tribute to that composer.

Danny Tercero, another figure of the Nicaraguan bolero, paid tribute to Los "Ángeles Negros", a Chilean group, on March 28, 2019, to commemorate the 51st anniversary of its creation.

The report was made by journalist Gloria Acosta, who explained that the singer performed the songs popularized by the Chilean group "Esta noche la paso contigo", "Como quiero decirte", "Mañana me iré", "No sufras más" and "Déjenme si estoy llorando".[xxxiv]

First International Bolero Festival, This event was held on February 13, 2013 on the occasion of Valentine's Day, patron saint of lovers.

A press release issued by Roger Solórzano Canales dated the day before, reported the presence of bolero singers from Cuba, Colombia, Mexico, El Salvador and Nicaragua.

The source explained that the event was organized by the Camerata Bach and the voices of Cuban Beatriz Márquez, Salvadoran Edmundo Alfaro, Colombian Beatriz Arellano, Mexican Lupina Cantú and Nicaraguans Luis Enrique Mejía Godoy, Eugenio Granera, Rebecka Molina and Rommel Ocampo were heard.

The festival was held at the Rubén Darío National Theater in Managua and the spectators enjoyed various expressions of the genre, such as traditional, bolero-jazz, trios and orchestras.

PARAGUAY

Despite the richness of its vernacular music, in this country the bolero has been expressed both in interpretation and in composition.

Classic boleros sound today at the Municipal Theater

On February 14, 2019, a special romantic musical evening for young and adult couples called La Noche del Bolero was held at the Municipal Theater of the capital of that country, with the participation of local musical groups.

Groups took to the stage that recalled the romantic evenings of the past, "*where the bride and groom danced on a tile*", performing classic compositions of the genre.

The participating groups were Rigoberto Arévalo and the Trio de Siempre, the Trio San Juan, Sajonia Cuatro, Tito Martínez, Kike Krona, Papilín Ayala with Los Garbos, and Pedro Perico López.

They performed, among others, the boleros "Somos novios", "En mi viejo San Juan", "Sin ti", "Amor de pobre", "Triunfamos", "Ladrona de besos", "La media vuelta", "Gema" "Estoy enamorado" and "Amor eterno", "El día que me quieras", "Adoro", "Contigo en la distancia", "Noelia", "Cantando al amor", "Estoy perdido", "Despierta", "Amor, qué malo eres", "Obsesión", "Amor, no fumes en la cama" and "Candilejas".

The Three South Americans were a musical trio formed in 1959 in Asunción, Paraguay and was made up of

Alma María Vaesken, Casto Darío Martínez and Johnny Torales.

That name was adopted when in 1959 they were summoned by Columbia, an Argentine record label, to record an LP in Buenos Aires. There they settled and traveled to Spain later where they were very popular

Among the songs performed are "Pájaro Campana", "Pájaro Chagüi", "Galopera", "Cuando caliente el sol", "El partido de fútbol", "Tómbola", "Quiero besar tus manos", "Cabellera negra", "Dulce penar", "Paloma blanca", "Nueva flor", "Luna asunceña", "Yo no sé por qué", "Sueño feliz", "Endúlzame", "Arráncame la vida", "Cuando salí de Cuba" and "Que suerte".

With the departure of Casto Darío, the trio disbanded.

Luis Guitarra fue el nombre artístico del músico, cantante y compositor *Luis Osmer Meza*, quien nació en Altos el 21 de junio de 1926 y falleció en Londres el 15 de septiembre de 1874. Es uno de los íconos de la música paraguaya.

He recorded more than 500 songs.

He performed at Madison Square in New York, the Olympia in Paris, the London Paladium, the Latin Quarter Tokyo, the Tchaikowsky in Moscow, and the Royal Variety Performance and Sanremo Festival in 1965

Some of the songs in his repertoire were "**Historia de un amor**", "**Buenas noches, mi amor**", "**Acuarela paraguaya**", "**Mi guitarra y mi voz**", "**Felicidades**", "**Adiós Mariquita Linda**" and "**Quizás, quizás, quizás**".

EL SALVADOR

This country has made a contribution to bolero both in interpretation and composition.

Álvaro Torres is the stage name of singer-songwriter *Álvaro Germán Ibarra Torres* who was born in Concepción Batres, Usulután, on April 9, 1954. Lyric baritone voice that began his professional activity in 1971.

Singer of ballads and boleros.

He composed his first song, "**Dulce amiga**", at the age of 12.

He is also the author of the songs: "Chiquita mía", "He vivo esperando por ti", "De punta a punta", "Hazme olvidarla", "Yo Te Seguiré queriendo", "Mi verdadero amor", "Si esfueras conmigo", "Te va a doler", "Tres", "Yo te seguiré queriendo", "Stress", "Ojalá", "Todo se paga", "Amor que mata", "Lo que se dice olvidar", "Reencuentro", "Nada se comparpara contigo", "Te olvidaré", "El Último Romántico", "A ti mi amor", "Al acecho", "Más romántico que nadie", "Ni tu ni ella", "Espacios vacíos", and "Aléjate de mí", among many others.

In 2006 he recorded with **José Feliciano** the songs "**No me vuelvo a enamorar**" and "**He viene a pedirte perdón**" included in the album Álvaro Torres Interpreta a Juan Gabriel en Boleros.

His work has earned him several gold and platinum awards.

While living in Guatemala he recorded his first albums entitled "Acaríciame", "Qué Lástima", "De Qué me Sirve Quererte" and "Ángel de Ternura".

CHILE

Bolero music in this country has relevant figures in interpretation and composition.

Ginette Acevedo is the stage name of singer *Mirna Jinett Acevedo Palma*, who was born in San Fernando, former province of Colchagua, on April 15, 1942.

On two occasions he won the Viña del Mar International Song Festival.

sHe recorded with the RCA Victor record labels in Chile, Argentina and Venezuela and Philips.

sHe popularized the songs **"Poema XX"**, **"Mis noches sin ti"**, **"Cariño malo"**, **"Arriba en la cordillera"**.

In 1962 the RCA Victor Chile record company recorded the album **"La voz de la ternura"**.

Rosamel Araya, stage name of singer *Héctor Rosamel Araya Plaza*, was born in San Antonio, Valparaíso Region, on August 30, 1936 and died in Buenos Aires, Argentina, on February 12, 1996.

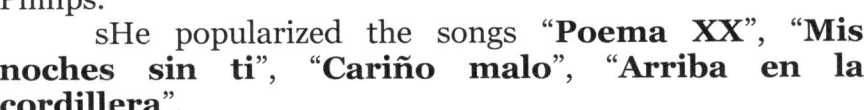

In 1958 he joined the group "Gatos Fantasmas", from Mendoza, Argentina, with which he toured first that country and then the rest of Latin America.

He settled in Argentina.

His main hits were the songs "Burn my eyes", "Repentant", "Our oath", "Two souls", "The broken cup", "Forbidden love", "Soul, heart and life", "You", "All a life", "Lamento borincano", "The ship of oblivion", "No", "Tears of the soul", "Private property" and "The letter".

Lucho Gatica was the stage name of singer, musician and composer *Luis Enrique Gatica Silva*, who was born in Rancagua on August 11, 1928 and died in Mexico City on November 13, 2018

He was called "***The King of Bolero***".

At the age of 18 he was introduced to the radio announcer Raúl Matas, moderator of the program La feria de los deseos, where he performed for the first time with the song "**Tú, donde estás**".

This same character made him meet in Santiago de Chile the Trio "Los Peregrinos", with whom he recorded the boleros "Contigo en la distancia" and "Sinceridad".

In 1953 he recorded, but with the orchestra of the British Maestro Roberto Inglez, his version of Consuelo Velázquez's song, "**Bésame mucho**".

Three years later he began a tour abroad that took him to Venezuela, In 1957, he decided to settle in Mexico, where he released the songs "**No me platiques**", "**Tú me acostumbraste**" and "**Voy a apagar la luz**".

In 1958, his first album was presented in LP format.

He popularized the bolero "**El Reloj**".

His incomplete discography includes the albums Inolvidables con Lucho, El gran Gatica and Encadenados (1958), Mis primeros éxitos (1964), Simplemente María (1976), 40 años cantle al amor (1992), Historia de un amor (2013) 50 canciones inmortales.

Palmenia Pizarro, is the stage name of the singer *Palmenia del Carmen Pizarro González*, who was born in San Felipe, Valparaíso Region, on July 19, 1941.

ShSe began his professional activities in 1961, he recorded with the labels EMI Music, Magic Records, Philips Records, Embassy, CBS, BMG, Sony Music, Feria Music

Website: www.palmeniapizarro.cl

At the age of 16, her participation in some radio stations in Santiago de Chile honored her with the mention "Best Folkloric Performer".

The song "**Cariño malo**", by the Peruvian composer Augusto Polo Campos, achieved its consecration.

During her stay in Mexico, with the help of Chavela Vargas, he made a great career that allowed him to perform in countries such as Australia, the United States, Argentina and Japan, where he recorded two songs in Japanese.

Her extensive discography is made up, among others, of the albums Un Corazón que canta, Palmenia, Siempre Palmenia, Sonríele a la vida, Boleros Inmortales, Reencuentro, Contigo viviré, 35 años de canto and "Reencuentro".

Antonio Prieto, stage name of the singer and film actor *Juan Antonio Prieto Espinoza*, who was born in Iquique on May 26, 1926, and died in Santiago de Chile on July 14, 2011.

In addition to Chile, he has worked in various Latin American and European countries.

He recorded more than a thousand songs. The best known was "**The Bride**".

It was active from 1949 to 2011.

His beginnings were in a popular radio show called La Feria de los Deseos, hosted by the well-known announcer Raúl Matas, on Radio Minería in Santiago de Chile, where he performed the song "**Tú ¿Dónde estás?**" that earned him instant recognition and allowed him to find his career.

In 1953 he was crooner of the Casino de Sevilla Orchestra in Spain, and with them Prieto recorded "**Las oscuras golondrinas**" and "**El mar y tú**".

His first success abroad was obtained in Argentina with the song "**Violetas imperiales**".[xxxv]

Los Ángeles Negros is a musical band founded in San Carlos (now Ñuble Region) in March 1968 by musicians **Cristián Blasser** and **Mario Gutiérrez**, who then recruited **Sergio Rojas** and **Germaín de la Fuente**. Since its creation, it quickly achieved international fame, but in 1973 a crisis began that led to the resignation of Germaín de la Fuente from the band in 1974 to continue a personal project in Mexico, called Germaín y Sus Ángeles Negros.

The rest of the group, then led by Nano Concha, with Luis Astudillo on drums and with the new vocalist, Ismael Montes, continued their career in Chile, keeping Mexico as one of their main places of presentation.

In 1982 it split again.

The group has performed in Ecuador, Peru, Uruguay, Paraguay, Bolivia, Colombia, part of Brazil, Venezuela, Central America, the United States, Canada, Puerto Rico, the Dominican Republic, Curaçao, Aruba and, finally, at the end of 1971, Mexico, where it established its domicile in 1982.

The band influenced various Latin American groups that emerged in the 1960s and 1970s. Among other musical groups, we can mention the Chileans Los Galos, Los Golpes or Capablanca, the Peruvians Los Pasteles Verdes and the Venezuelans Los Terrícolas. During the 1990s, the band also influenced new Mexican groups, belonging to the grupero genre, that emerged on the border with the United States.

From its different stages are the albums that follow: Because I love you, And I will return, I want more of you,

Tonight I spend it with you, The appointment, The train to oblivion, Leave me if I'm crying, Stay in my dreams, Applaud my end, My life like a carousel, Despacito, Serenade without a moon, Passion and life, Locamente mine, Whole a life, The long-awaited return and Metamorphosis, among others.[xxxvi]

PERÚ

This country contributed to the history of popular music the Bolero Cantinero, as well as emblematic figures of the genre both in the field of composition and in interpretation.

Los Pasteles Verdes was founded in 1970 in Chimbote and was originally made up of *Aldo Guibovich* (vocals), *Hugo Acuña Lecca* (guitar), *César Acuña* (keyboards), *Miguel Moreno* (bass), *Ernesto Pozo* (drums), *Raúl Padilla* (percussions) and *Germán Laos* (tropical singer), all students of the San Pedro school, where they took their first musical steps, becoming a sensation among schoolmates and friends.

The foregoing data, like those that follow, were extracted from *Wikipedia, the free encyclopedia*.

After numerous minor presentations at parties and festivals, the source points out, on October 13, 1973, the directors of INFOPESA, the record company with the greatest projection in Peru at that time, gave them the opportunity to record two songs, "**Puertos Queridos**" (tropical), performed by Germán Laos, and "**Angelitos Negros**".

The success forced the label to produce the group's first LP with songs such as: "**El reloj**", "**Recuerdos de una noche**" and "**El presidiario**" with which they reaffirmed their triumph. With the first he achieved the first Gold Record.

These were some of his albums: "Recuerdos de una Noche", "Con mucho amor", "Mañana de amor", "Mi amor imposible", "Ámame", "Amame", "Esclavo y amo", "Los

Pasteles Verdes en USA", "Ruega por nosotros", "15 Éxitos de Los Pasteles Verdes" and "Corazón solitario".xxxvii

Pedro Otiniano, stage name of *Pedro Otiniano Chiesa*, who was born in Lima on March 27, 1937, and died in the same city on August 2, 2012.

He was called "**The Nightingale of Love**" and also "**Pedrito Otiniano**". At the age of 9 he performed the Peruvian waltz "Fatalidad" on Radio Mundial and at 19 he won a festival on Radio Excelsior that marked his path to the bolero cantinero.

He was part of the trios: "Continental" and "Los Troveros".

He recorded more than 600 boleros and sang in Portuguese, Spanish and Japanese.

His repertoire was formed, among others, by the songs "Cinco centavitos", "Ay cariño", "Tres amores", "Toda una vida", "Vida de mi vida", "Que te vaya bien", "Mil amores", "Pintor" and "Doce campanadas".

Lucho Barrios, singer and composer, was born in El Callao on April 22, 1935 and died in Lima on May 5, 2010.

He formed the trio "Los Incas", of ephemeral life.

He traveled to Ecuador at the invitation of **Julio Jaramillo**.

He recorded singles with the Smith record label.

In addition to Ecuador, he performed successfully in Chile, France. In Peru he signed with the MAG record label, recording successful songs such as "Marabú", "Me engañas mujer", "Mentirosa", "Te alejas", "Copas de licor", "Mala", "Adúltera", "Mirando y sonriendo", "Borrasca", "Nido de amor" and many more. He also recorded with Sono Radio, but it was with IEMPSA that he recorded most of his great songs, such as "Oh pintor", "El retrato de mamá", "Dos medallitas",

"Mi viejo", "Amor de pobre", "No me amenaces", "Cruel condena", "El día más hermoso" and the reissue of his hit "Marabú", as well as a variety of LPs on the Odeón Iempsa label.

In 1961, he returned to Chile, in whose capital he recorded his first Long Play, growing even more his fame in that country, Argentina, Mexico, and even in the United States.

He was called "**The King of Bolero**" and "**Mister Marabú**".

This is how the newspaper Vanguardia of Mexico reported his death on May 5, 2010 :

Lucho Barrios, composer of "Mi niña bonita", dies

Lima, Peru. - Peruvian singer and songwriter Luis "Lucho" Barrios, author of songs such as "Mi niña bonita", died here today, two days after suffering a massive heart attack and pulmonary thrombosis, medical sources reported.

Barrios was admitted last Monday to the intensive care unit of the 2 de Mayo Hospital, where he died on Wednesday.

Known as "Lucho", Barrios was born in the capital's port of El Callao, on April 22, 1935, where he grew up until he was nine years old and then lived on Penitencia Street, in the Barrios Altos area, cradle of great artists and performers.

He studied at the National School of Opera, was part of the folkloric group Pacha Mama, was in the trio Los Incas and then as a soloist recorded singles with the Smith record label.

He shared musical concerns with the Ecuadorian singer Julio Jaramillo, who invited him to sing in Ecuador and one of his first hits was the waltz "Juanita".

In Peru he recorded the boleros entitled "Marabú", "Me engañas mujer", "Mentirosa", "Te alejas" and "Copas de licor", among others, and with his hits he toured several countries of the continent.

En Chile, Lucho Barrio grabó, entre muchos otros temas, "La joya del Pacífico", del compositor chileno Víctor Acosta, que se convirtió en un verdadero himno del puerto de Valparaíso.

En el año 2002 el gobierno del presidente chileno Ricardo Lagos lo condecoró por ser un artista peruano ejemplar, por su gran aporte a la música popular y su fuerte arraigo entre el pueblo chileno.

"Lucho" Barrios, quien recibió además un premio de la Organización de Estados Americanos (OEA) por su trabajo en favor del acercamiento de los pueblos a través del canto, tenía como su tema favorito "Mi niña bonita", la cual dedicó a todas las mujeres del mundo.

Trío "Los Morunos". In its first period, which lasted from 1961 to 1974, it was made up of *Manuel Ortiz, Guillermo Medina* and *Alfredo Aguirre.*

He recorded his first 45 rpm and LP hits on Sono Radio and won the Trujillo Festival with the bolero "**Yo volveré**". His songs became fashionable, and he made presentations throughout the Peruvian territory. They were, in addition to the previous one, among others, "Adelante", "Egoísta", "Cien Puñales", "Yo te quiso", "Mi perdición", "Osito de felpa" and "Shua".

In 1974 the trio performed at the El Tambo Tourist Restaurant and there they were hired to perform in Toronto, Canada. That same year Guillermo Medina traveled to New York where he took up residence; Alfredo Aguirre returned to

Peru and formed the quartet Los Hnos. Aguirre and Manuel Ortiz became part of the Los Panchos Trio in 1976.

The new stage of the trio began in 1978 and had Manuel Ortiz, Modesto Pastor and Luis Silva as members.

Los Hermanos Castro is a musical group that began in 1969 as a duo of siblings *Elvia* and *Lucho Castro* and when they appeared on the radio program "Trampolín a la fama" with their song "**Igual que Magdalena**" and there began the musical takeoff.

Later, Benito Castro, Gualberto Castro and Arturo Castro, Shessira, Marlon, Karlos and Luigi joined.

Among the main songs in her repertoire are "Con tinta roja", "Justo ahora me olvidas", ¿A qué has venido?!, "Igual que Magdalena", "Triste me voy", "Lléname más la copa", "Y nunca más", "La del vestido de novia", "Por nada del mundo", "Luto en el alma" and "Todo por nada".

In September 2019, on the occasion of the group's 49th anniversary, two new productions appeared with unreleased songs, one and the other with a compilation of their greatest hits.

On that occasion it was directed by Lucho Castro and was made up of his sons Marlon, Shessira and Luigui.[xxxviii]

Johnny Farfán is the stage name of singer and composer *Julio Gárate Farfán*, who was born in Lima on January 17, 1943.

He is called the "***Elegant Voice of the Bolero***" and is considered one of the three great founders of this musical current in that country, along with Lucho Barrios and Pedrito Otiniano.

His songs, already classics, are: "Señor Abogado", "El oro de tu pelo", "Ñatita", "Humo y licor", "Por qué un himno de paz", "El brillo de tus ojos", "Déjame ver una vez más", "Mi niña de ayer" and the well-known "Se llama María" among others.[xxxix]

Iván Cruz is the stage name of singer, composer and musician *Víctor Francisco de la Cruz Dávila*, who was born in El Callado on January 10, 1946
He is called "***The Idol of Bolero***".
Among his compositions are "Me dices que te vas", "Vagabundo", "Ajena" and "Yo le doy Gracias a Dios".
He began his career in 1973 as a ballad singer until, in 1975, the artistic director of the FTA label (RCA Victor), Marco Antonio Collazos, recommended that he start singing boleros, recording his first two singles: "**Me dices que te vas**" and "**Mozo, deme otra copa**".
His work has been rewarded with several gold and platinum records.
He recorded ten albums in Peru and three in Venezuela and around 200 singles.
In 2015, the record label Infopesa, published an album entitled El Disco de Oro, where his most emblematic songs are compiled.[xl]

Gaby Zevallos, singer, was born in El Callao on an undetermined date in 1948 and died in Lima on July 11, 2016.
She was called "***The Queen of Bolero***" and is a historical reference of the Peruvian bolero.
Gaby Zevallos, the Peruvian who brought Juan Gabriel's hits to the bolero
In 1997 he recorded a CD with songs by **Juan Gabriel**, distributed by a national newspaper. It consisted of 13 of the most popular songs of the famous Mexican singer-songwriter with songs such as "Amor eterno", "Costumbres", "Así fue",

"Frente a frente" and "Hasta que te conocí" among other great hits.

She became known on a radio program of new voices directed by who would later be her husband and manager.

"Tenga cuidado señora", by Alejandro Laguna, was one of his last recordings; however, his audience continued to ask him for the classic songs. "Ese hombre", "Popurrí homenaje a Virginia López", "Que me perdonen los dos", "Acepto mi destino", "Mi súplica", "Penumbra", "El amor y el querer", "Me gustas" and "Ella" among others, in addition to the songs of Juan Gabriel.

Her most remembered songs are "Señora", "Ella" and "Mal hombre", but the one that had the highest sales was "Corazón Herido", recorded on the Infopesa label.[xli]

Guiller, stage name of *Guillermo Caldas*, singer and composer. He is known in the world of bolero cantinero as Guiller, "***El Rey de las Cantinas***". Author, among others, of the boleros cantineros "**Qué pena**", "**Pregúntate**" and "**Pronto partiré**".[xlii]

ARGENTINA

Despite the roots of tango, this country has made great contributions to bolero music, both in singing and in composition. Some important figures of the Argentine bolero universe are the following:

Carlos Argentino, stage name of singer *Israel Vitenszteim Vurm*, who was born in Buenos Aires on June 23, 1929 and died in the same city on June 20, 1991. Initially he used the pseudonym Carlos Torres. He was known as **"The King of the Charanga"**.

He began his professional career in the orchestras of Luis Rolero and Raúl Marengo performing in Peru and Chile. He then traveled to Colombia with the Efraín Orozco orchestra.

It reads in Wikipedia, the free encyclopedia that *"Something very curious happened on that trip, since there was a Colombian singer named Carlos Torres, and in order to differentiate himself, his patronymic was added, remaining as Carlos Torres Argentino, and then consecrated artistically as Carlos Argentino"*.

He also traveled to Havana in 1952, where he worked with the orchestras of Felo Bergaza, Arnoldo Nalli and Julio Cuevas and finally joined the Orquesta Sonora Matancera, with which he recorded his first 78 rpm album on August 17, 1956.

Among his bolero interpretations are the titles **"Alma vendida"**, **"No pidas más perdón"**, **"Cruel indiferencia"**, "El amor no existe" and **"Cuando tú seas mía"**.[xliii]

Manuela Bravo is a singer and actress born on January 12, 1954, in the city of La Plata.

Their first single album was called "El fruto de nuestro amor". With the song "**A que no te vas**" she won the Third National and International Song Festival, in Buga (Colombia).

She participated in the Feria del Milagro, Ecuador, along with Julio Iglesias and Raphael. In New York she won with the song "**Me está gustando**", which was on New York television for a month.

In 1976, the record company CBS released his album Bésame mucho, which includes hit songs such as: "Hoy", "Amor y duda", and "Me está gustando", among others.

The same company later released her album "A mi manera".

She also recorded the albums "Manuela Bravo", "Ámame ahora con la lluvia", "Vivir", "Zona prohibida", "Persona a persona", "20 secretos de amor" and "Hablo de vivir", among many others.

Horacio Casares, stage name of singer and actor *Ignacio Andrés Mobilio*, who was born in Buenos Aires on September 26, 1932 and died in the same city on August 25, 2009.

He was called "***El Galán Cantor***". In addition to bolero, he also sang tango.

He made artistic tours of Peru, Chile, Uruguay, Mexico and Brazil.

Among his songs are: "Hasta siempre amor", "Llámame amor mío", "Lloremos", "Flor de lino", "Cuándo, Cuándo, Cuándo", "Mensajero", "Envidias", "Siete notas", "Un desolado corazón" and "Cuando llega el fin del mundo".

Mario Clavell is the stage name of singer, actor, musician and composer *Miguel Mario Clavell*, who was born in Ayacucho on October 9, 1922, and died in Buenos Aires on March 10, 2011.

He made her debut at the age of 9 as a soloist at the End of Years party of the San José School, in Tandil and in the choir of the Parish Church.

At the age of 18 he began professionally as a crooner in the jazz group of Adolfo Carabelli, on Radio Belgrano with the pseudonym of Mario Clawell. He then worked for a major insurance company.

In 1944 he premiered one of his first songs and then, thanks to the Mexican Juan Arvizu, it was presented at the Julio Korn Publishing House, where he made his first publishing contracts.

His greatest hits were performed by various singers and orchestras in the country such as Leo Marini, Gregorio Barrios, Libertad Lamarque and Pedro Vargas.

In his beginnings as an author, he stood out with the songs "¿Por qué?", "¿Qué será de mí?", "Hasta siempre", "Porque tú lo quieres", "Mi carta", "Somos" and "Abrázame así".

His artistic work was recognized with various distinctions.

Alberto Cortez is the stage name of *José Alberto García Gallo*, singer-songwriter and guitarist, who was born in Rancui, La Pampa, on March 11, 1940 and died in Madrid, Spain, on April 4, 2019.

His best-known songs are, among others, "En un rincón del alma", "Cuando un amigo se va",

"Callejero", "Mi árbol y yo", "A partir de mañana", "Manolo", "Te llega una rosa", "Castillos en el aire" and "El abuelo".

With singer-songwriter Facundo Cabral he recorded four albums and made successful tours of Latin America.

His discography exceeded 40 albums, including Boleros, Poemas y canciones, Lo mejor de Alberto Cortez, Poemas y canciones, two volumes, Distancia, No soy de aquí, Pensares y sentires and No soy de aquí.

Leo Marini is the stage name of singer and actor *Alberto Batet Vitali*, who was born in Mendoza on August 23, 1920, and died in the same city on October 15, 2000.

It was active from 1942 to 1999, it was called "**The Voice that caresses**".

He recorded with the Odeón and Seeco Records labels.

His first performance was on the radio station of Mendoza.

With a group of friends, in 1941 he traveled to Chile, where he was hired to sing in dance halls and radio stations in Valparaíso and Viña del Mar.

Later an artistic tour took him, in 1948, to Venezuela, Cuba, Puerto Rico, the Dominican Republic and again Venezuela. He made a new tour, this time through Peru, Ecuador and Colombia, where he witnessed the Bogotazo.

In 1978 he was decorated by the then president of Venezuela, Carlos Andrés Pérez, along with Libertad Lamarque, Toña la Negra, Bobby Capó, Dámaso Pérez Prado and Pedro Vargas.

In that country in 1980, Renato Capriles, director of the dance orchestra "Los Melódicos", requested his services as guest vocalist on the first album of the Orquesta La Grande.

His repertoire was made up, among many others, of the boleros "Virgen de medianoche", "Llanto de luna", "Ya lo verás", "Caribe soy", "Puedes irte de mí" "Inútilmente", "Cerca de ti" and "Yo contigo me voy".

He was part of the Sonora Matancera orchestra, and the first song recorded with the group was "Luna yumurina", followed by "Quiero un trago tabernero", "Mi desolación" and "Desde que te vi".

Chico Novarro is the stage name of singer-songwriter *Bernardo Mitnik*, who was born in Santa Fe on September 4, 1934.

He began his professional career in 1955 and has recorded on the RCA Victor labels, CBS, Microfon, Polygram (Philips) and Suramusic.

In the field of pop music, he was part of the cast of the Club del Clan from 1962 to 1964. He is the author of almost six hundred songs, plays and music for shows and films.

In addition to bolero, he sings jazz, rock, pop and cumbia.

In 1965 he wrote his first tango, "**Nuestro balance**", with which he won at the Festival del Parque del Plata in Uruguay.

Among his compositions are "Algo contigo", "Un sábado más" and "Cuenta conmigo", a song that won the OTI festival in 1979, performed by Daniel Riolobos.

His songs have also been interpreted, among others, by the singers José José and Tito Rodríguez who also interpreted in bolero his tangos "Nuestro balance", "Como" and "El último acto".

His discography includes, among many other albums, the titles "Alegre y romántico", "Algo contigo", "Arráncame la vida", "El amor continua", "La noche", "Mi mayor amor" and "Grandes Éxitos".

Eduardo Farrel, was a singer who was born in Buenos Aires on an unestablished date of 1920 and died in the same city on June 21, 1997.

He performed on stages in Mexico, Venezuela, Peru, Cuba, Puerto Rico, Jamaica, Trinidad and Tobago, Colombia, Martinique and the United States, where he recorded an English version of "El Choclo".

In Argentina she sang with **Roberto Yanés** on Channel 9.

He had a degree in chemistry.

In 1943 he made his first recording with the René Cóspito orchestra: containing the songs "**Queja Caribe**" and "**Al Compás del Ritmo**".

He was an exclusive artist for Radio Belgrano and Radio Splendid.

Most of his songs were recorded by the Odeón and Music Hall record labels.

These were some of his hits: "Nada más", "Quiéreme mucho", "Quisiera ser tu canción", "Dos almas", "Hablemos clara", "La noche es nuestra", "Beso", "Reloj", "El Choclo", "Pasito", "Mariquilla Bonita", "Toda una vida", "Nosotros" and "Hoja seca".

Raúl Carrell, stage name of singer and actor *Oscar Raúl de Cicco*, who was born in Buenos Aires on November 28, 1926 and died in the same city on October 21, 2003.

He was called "***The Last Romantic***."

He recorded with the Odeon and Music Hall labels.

He made his debut as a singer in Carlos Marcucci's orchestra under the pseudonym Raúl **Morel**, but his time in tango, then, was fleeting.

In 1949 he turned to the melodic genre, replacing Carlos Argentino in the Dajos Bela orchestra.

He replaced Hernán Avilés in the Los Panchos Trio due to illness and was very popular abroad.

In Caracas, for example, he was accompanied by Agustín Lara and his decision to turn to romantic music was imposed on him by a piece of advice from José Mojica.

He recorded 14 albums and with the bolero he toured the world being awarded important prizes, remaining six years on the bill in Brazil where he sang with the orchestras of Luis Bonfá, Roberto Inglez and Héctor Lagna Fietta, and causing a real sensation in Portugal.

The source consulted does not indicate his discography or his successes.

Palito Ortega is the stage name *Ramón Bautista Ortega*, of the singer-songwriter, actor, record producer, film director and politician, who was born in Lules, Tucumán, on March 8, 1941.

From the 1960s he was a member of the musical group El Club del Clan, which had a relevant impact and remained for several years.

Between 1991 and 1995 he served as governor of Tucumán and between 1995 and 2000 he was a senator for the same province.

He has filmed 33 films and as a singer she sold more than 28 million records of her hits "**Despeinada**" and "**La felicidad**".

His extensive discography, recorded almost entirely by the RCA Victor label, includes among many other albums the titles "Palito Ortega", "Palito siempre primero ", "Internacional", "Canta boleros en Río", "Mi primera novia", "Impacto", "Un muchacho como yo", "El magnetismo de Palito Ortega", "El creador", "Muchacho de oro", "Viva la vida", "Un canto a la vida", "Me gusta ser como soy", "El Fenomeno", "La Sonrisa de mama".

The same label made the following compilations: "Lo mejor de Palito Ortega", "Corazón contento", "Canciones románticas", "Lo mejor de Palito Ortega, dos volúmenes" and "Ayer, hoy y siempre".

Daniel Riolobos is the stage name of singer *Pedro Nicasio Riolobos*, who was born in Godoy Cruz, Mendoza, on December 14, 1932, and died in Mexico on June 17, 1992.

He sang for the first time on the radio at the age of five. He was in Chile, where he began to perform as crooner of the orchestra conducted by Roberto Inglez until he replaced the Chilean Lucho Gatica. Thanks to the success obtained, he launched himself as a soloist in Venezuela, Cuba, Puerto Rico, the United States and Mexico, where he settled in 1958.

His discography consists, among other titles, of the albums "La voz de América", "A Tropical Evening with Daniel Riolobos", "Solo pienso en ti", "Romántico", "El día que me quieras", "Por y para mis amigos", "La música de ayer, hoy y siempre", "La voz y la personality de Daniel Riolobos", "Los Éxitos de Daniel Riolobos", "De hombre a hombre", "Grandes Exitos", "La noche de anoche", "Romantically Tuyo" and "20 Secretos de Amor".

Elio Roca is the stage name of singer-songwriter, actor and politician *Roberto Orlando Bracone Macceiali*, who was born in Sáenz Peña, Chaco on July 31, 1943.

He released her debut album, Bella, bionda, Carina, in 1965. He is known for the singles "I Wish to Be Your Love," "I Need You So Much, Love," and "I Want to Draw You."

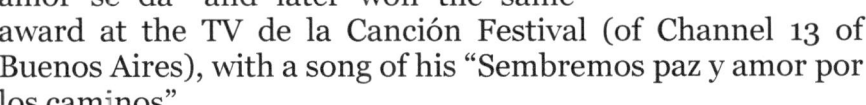

He debuted at the age of 7, singing in the television program Ronda infantil.

In 1966 the record company Polydor released the album El mundo de Elio Roca, where he recorded the songs "Nadie me puede juzgar" and "El amor".

In 1970 he won the first prize at the Punta del Este Festival (Uruguay), with a song of his authorship, "Cuando el amor se da" and later won the same award at the TV de la Canción Festival (of Channel 13 of Buenos Aires), with a song of his "Sembremos paz y amor por los caminos".

That same year he recorded very successful songs such as "El triste", "Cómo deseo ser tu amor" and "Otra vez junto a ti".

In 1992 he recorded the bolero album "De mil amores".

His discography, almost all recorded by the Polydor label, consists among others of the albums "Elio Roca", "El mundo de Elio Roca", "Poema de amor", "Yo canto", "Vas a pensar en mí", "Por finré logra tener tu amor", "Contigo y aquí", "Porque te quiero, es mi única verdad", "Mientras pasa el tiempo" and "Te extrañaré donde estés"

Sandro is the stage name of the singer-songwriter, film director, actor and guitarist, *Roberto Sánchez Ocampo*, who was born in Buenos Aires on August 19, 1945 and died on January 4, 2010 in Guaymallén, Mendoza.

He was called "***Sandro de América***".

In 2005 he won the Latin Grammy Award for Musical Excellence and recorded 52 original albums.

His most successful songs were, among many others: "Dame el fuego de tu amor", "Rosa Rosa", "Quiero llenarme de ti", "Penumbras", "Porque yo te amo", "Así", "Mi amigo el Puma", "Tengo", "Trigal and "Una muchacha y una guitarra".

Likewise, during his career he made 16 films, and was also the first Latin American to sing in the Felt Forum room of Madison Square Garden.

Among his main albums are the titles:

"Introducing Sandro" (1964) released in 1998. It contains the singles released prior to his first album "Sandro y Los de Fuego" (1965), "Al calor de Sandro y Los de Fuego" (1966), "El surprising mundo de Sandro" (1966), "Alma y fuego" (1966), "Beat Latino" (1967), "Quiero llenarme de ti" (1968), "Una muchacha y una guitarra" (1968), "La magia de Sandro" (1968), "Sandro después de diez años" (1973), "Sandro... Siempre Sandro" (1974), "Para mamá" (2001). "Mi vida, mi música" (2003), "Amor gitano (2004) and Secretamente palabras de amor" (2006).

Roberto Yanés is the stage name of singer-songwriter, pianist and actor *Roberto César Iannacone*, who was born in Villa de María del Río Seco, province of Córdoba on April 25, 1932 and died in Buenos Aires on May 30, 2019.

During his childhood he sang on the radio and then studied music at the Provincial Conservatory of Music. During his military service, he gave presentations at the officers' casino.

In 1958 he signed as a solo artist with the CBS label. With this label he recorded "Dónde será mi vida" and "El espejo", songs that achieved relative success.

In 1963 he recorded with Astor Piazzolla an EP with the songs "Cafetín de Buenos Aires", "Margarita Gauthier", "Fuimos" and "Griseta".

His repertoire also included the songs "Camino del puente", "Si me comprendieras", "Volver", "Contigo en la distancia" and "El reloj".

He authored the songs "Querer como nadie" and "Te desafío".

He recorded 80 albums, including the albums "Corazón a corazón", "Momentos íntimos", "Un poquito", "La última cita", "Cualquiera" and "En la intimidad".

PUERTO RICO

After Cuba and Mexico, this country is the one that produced the most bolero singers, composers and musical groups.

Johnny Albino is the name of singer and guitarist *Juan Antonio Albino Ortiz* who was born in Yauco and died in New York on May 7, 2011.

He was active from 1946 to 1995.

In 1946, he formed his first Trio San Juan with Jaime Gozilez, lead guitar, and José Ramón Ortiz, second vocals. The group debuted in New York City. However, Albino's rise to fame came as a vocalist with some of the most famous trios of that era.

With the San Juan Trio, he sang well-known and now classic songs, such as "Cosas como tú", "No sigamos pecando", "Plazos traicioneros", "Vuelve Cuando Quieres" and "Por el bien de los dos"

He was part of the Los Panchos Trio and also worked with stars such as Frank Sinatra, Sammy Davis, Eydie Gormé, Xavier Gugat, Nat King Cole and Steve Lawrence. He also worked with, including two albums they recorded together, without the rest of the trio.

His discography includes more than 300 albums. He has performed numerous concert tours around the world in places such as Japan, Hong Kong, Singapore, Egypt, Israel, and throughout Europe and Latin America.

Chucho Avellanet is the stage name of singer and actor *Armando Hipólito Avellanet González*, who was born in Mayagüez on August 13, 1941.

His first formal performance was as the opening act for Myrta Silva, at the Tropicoro Room of the San Juan Hotel in Carolina, Puerto Rico.

His first album was titled Fugitiva. "Magia blanca" was  his first hit. Around that time, he recorded Fugitiva, his first album. Her first hit was "Magia blanca", a Spanish version of the song Devil Woman by Marty Robbins and later achieved international projection with "Jamás te olvidaré", a version of I Can't Stop Loving You.

With the United Artist record label, he recorded 15 productions. He also recorded with the labels DiscoHit, RicoVox, El Palacio de la Música (Venezuela), Velvet de Venezuela, Velvet de Puerto Rico, TH Records, Artomax Studio, InnerCat Music Group and Apollo Music.

Hernando Avilés is the stage name of singer, songwriter and guitarist *Herminio Avilés Negrón*, who was  born in San Juan, Puerto Rico on February 1, 1914, and died in Mexico City on July 26, 1986.

He was active from 1937 to 1986.

His professional career began in 1932 when he was part of the Los Antillanos Trio, then the Los Gauchos Trio and then the Las Tres Guitarras Trio. From 1941 to 1944 he formed the Dueto Azteca together with the Mexican singer Sotero San Miguel. He was also a soloist with several orchestras.

In 1944 he formed in New York, together with Alfredo Gil and Chucho Navarro, the Trio Los Panchos, of which he was the first voice.

In 1952 he formed the Avilés Quartet and six years later he joined the Los Tres Reyes Trio.

Bobby Capó is the stage name of singer, musician and composer *Félix Manuel Rodríguez Capó*, who was born in San Juan, Puerto Rico on January 1, 1921 and died in Barcelona, Spain, on December 18, 1989.

One of his best-known compositions is the bolero "Piel canela". He is also the author of the songs "Y llorando me dormí", "Luna de miel en Puerto Rico" and "Soñando con Puerto Rico".

His artistic career began when for fortuitous reasons he had to replace the singer Davilita in the Victoria Quartet. However, his fame began when he recorded as a soloist with the orchestra of the well-known Spanish musician Xavier Cugat.

He was a member of the Cuban orchestra Sonora Matancera.

He recorded the following albums: 1958 – "Bobby Capó Sings", 1958 – "Yo Canto Para Ti", 1964 – "Love Songs of Rafael Hernandez", 1968 – "Invitation to Love", 1970 – "Despierte Borincano", 1973 – "La música de Puerto Rico", 1976 – "Simply... Amor", 1980 – "Luna de Miel en Puerto Rico", 1986, "50th anniversary Goya", 1998 – with La Sonora Matancera.

Cheo Feliciano is the stage name of singer and musician *José Luis Feliciano Vega*, who was born in Ponce on July 3, 1935 and died in San Juan, Puerto Rico on April 17, 2014.

He was called "***The Spoiled Child of Puerto Rico***."

He was active from 1957 to 2014.

He recorded on the labels Seeco Records, Fania Records, RMM and Universal Music.

In addition to being a bolero singer, he was a salsa singer.

In New York he belonged to Joe Cuba's sextet and between 1967 and 1969 he was part of Eddie Palmieri's group as vocalist.

In 1983 he founded his own label called Coche Records, with an ephemeral life.

He then signed with RMM Records & Video, recording five albums. Subsequently, he reached an agreement with the Venezuelan group La Rondalla Venezolana and the Venezuelan record label Palacio de la Música to record the album "Son inolvidables" (1995).

Charlie Figueroa is a singer whose biography does not appear on the Web, which only indicates that he died in New York on October 25, 1955 and was a member of the Cuarteto Bambú and a musical group of Daniel Santos.

The source adds that he was one of the great voices of the Puerto Rican bolero and that part of his repertoire was made up of the songs "Tú serás mía", "Culpa al destino", "Cómo tú reías", "Busco tu recuerdo", "La vida es un sueño", "Celos sin razón", "Madrigal", "Estar Contigo", "Por eso me voy", "El último suspiro", "No pises mi camino".

Other texts on the Web reveal that it was the first of a style followed by singers such as Daniel Santos and that its first six recordings in its order were with the following groups: Conjunto Típico Ladi, Orquesta Arturo Somohano and Orquesta Carmelo Díaz Soler.[xliv]

Daniel Santos is the stage name of singer-songwriter *Daniel Doroteo de los Santos Betancourt* who was born in

Santurce on February 5, 1916 and died in Ocala, Florida, United States, November 27, 1992.

In 1938, while working in a casino in Manhattan, he sang the song "**Amor perdido**" without knowing that its composer, Pedro Flores, was in the audience. Flores loved the performance and invited Daniel to join his group "El Cuarteto Flores".

In 1941, he recorded one of his greatest hits, "**Despedida**", also by Pedro Flores, which was banned from the radio.

He was part of the Cuban orchestra Sonora Matancera.

In addition to the two previous songs, he also successfully performed, among many others, the boleros "Virgen de medianoche", "Nuestro Juramento", "Perdón", "Linda", "Esperanza inútil" and "Amor".

He also performed plenas and guarachas.

José Luis Moneró, singer and musician who was born in Junco on April 6, 1921 and died on February 15, 2011 in Caguas.

He was called "***The Prince of the Antillean Song***".

He was part of the orchestras of Alberto Iznaga, Don Maya, Rafael Muñoz, Noro Morales, José Curbelo and Xavier Cugat. He also had his own musical group, the Original Super Orchestra.

He is considered the last of the great Puerto Rican bolero singers of the Golden Age of the romantic song of his native country.

His album Doce Canciones y Un Millón de Recuerdos included his hits, "Olvídame," "Sin rumbo," "Añoranza," "Mi loca tentación," "Inconsolable," "Sin ti," "Pétalos de rosa," "Un viejo amor," "No me mires así," "Caminos de ayer," "Ensueños" and "Lena."[xlv]

Carmen Delia Dipiní, singer who was born in Naguabo, on November 18, 1927, and died in Bayamón on August 4, 1998.

She was part of the Cuban orchestra Sonora Matancera, where she achieved his greatest successes.

She began singing in 1937, under the instruction of teacher Amparo Brenes of the Eugenio Brac Elementary School in Naguabo, but her debut was in 1941 in a program that Rafael Quiñones Vidal hosted on the WNAM radio station.

In New York she became a professional singer when she was participating in Willy Chevalier's amateur program at the Triboro Theater, and won a First Prize and the Verne record company hired her to record with Johnny Albino and the San Juan Trio the songs "El día que nací yo", "Perdida" and "Duérmete mi Junior". Later she was hired by the Casa Seeco and with them she recorded "Besos de fuego", a tango whose original title is "El choclo" and which, with a new lyric by Mario de Jesús, accompanied by the René Touzet Orchestra, catapulted her internationally.

She also sang with the Casino Ensemble and did radio and television in Havana. He joined Johnny Rodríguez and reaped countless hits with the songs "Fichas negras", "Soy mimosa" and "Dímelo".

She also recorded other great hits such as "Son amores", "Experiencia", "Si no vuelves", "Delirio", "Amor perdido", "Congoja" and "No es venganza". Throughout his life he recorded 30 full-length albums.

Virginia López is the stage name of *Dolores Virginia Rivera García*, who was born in New York on November 29, 1928. She is considered Puerto Rican because she was raised by a family of emigrants from that country.

She was known as **"The Voice of Tenderness"** and **"The Puerto Rican"**.

Among her albums are Virginia López, three volumes: "Azul Pintado de azul", "Canta Virginia López", "Tesoros de corazón", "20 Éxitos de Virginia López" and "Éxitos De Oro".

His most successful boleros were "Cariñito azucarado", "¡Te odio y te quiero!", "Osito de felpa" and "Por equivocación"

Recording for RCA Victor, Mexico became his international launching pad. Thus his voice spread in Latin America, some countries in Europe and Japan.

He recorded with mariachis, orchestras, ensembles, as well as with his inseparable Trio Imperio.

In Mexico she was distinguished with the Golden Discómetro and in Puerto Rico she was awarded an award from the Festival de Elbows.[xlvi]

Rafael Hernández is the stage name of musician and composer *Rafael Hernández Marín*, who was born in Aguadilla on October 24, 1891, and died in San Juan, Puerto Rico on December 11, 1965.

He was a player of cornet, violin, trombone, euphonium, guitar and piano.

At the age of 12 he studied music in San Juan, under the direction of music teachers José Ruellan Lequenica and Jesús Figueroa, and at 14 he played for the Cocolía Orchestra.

His musical legacy rises to more than two thousand compositions of all genres, among which are: "Lamento Borincano", the best known, "Silencio", "Amor, no me quieres tanto", "Espérame en el cielo", "Ausencia", "Perfume de gardenias", "Capullito de alelí", "Canción del alma", "Amor ciego", "Por tu amor", "Lo siento por ti", "Diez años", "Campanitas de Cristal", "Desvelo de Amor", "Preciosa" and "El Cumbanchero".

"**Lamento Borincano**" has been performed, among many others, by Alfonzo Ortiz Tirado, Gilberto Santa Rosa, Marc Anthony, La India, Javier Solís, Chavela Vargas, José Feliciano, Luis Fonsi and Víctor Jara. His composition "**Qué chula es Puebla**" is considered the regional anthem of the Mexican state of the same name. A handlebar was erected there. Similarly, "**Linda Qisquella**" is considered by many Dominicans to be a second anthem.

Pedro Flores, is the stage name of the composer and musician *Pedro Flores Córdova*, who was born in Naguabo on April 9, 1894 and died in San Juan on July 14, 1979.

In 1926 he settled in New York where he met the composer Rafael Hernández with whom he became a great friend and although he had no academic musical training, he was collaborating with him and his group: the Trio Borinquen.

In 1930 he formed his own group: Cuarteto Flores.

Later he moved to Mexico, then to Cuba and on occasion returned to New York to reorganize his group, with the collaboration of Daniel Santos, Los Panchos, La Sonora Matancera, Myrta Silva, Clarisa Perea, Moncho Usera, Doroteo Santiago and Chencho Moraza, with whom he made important tours of the American continent.

In 1967 he returned to Puerto Rico and continued to compose songs,

His first two songs, composed in 1926, were called "Toma jabón pa' que te laves" and "El jilguero" and the best known are "Perdón", "Esperanza inútil", "Bajo un palmar", "Obsesión", "¿Qué te pasa?", "Ay, qué bueno!", "Borracho, no vale", "Sin bandera", "Se vende una casita", "Venganza", "Amor perdido", "Despedida", "Celos", "Linda", "Si no eres tú", "Qué extraña es la vida", "Margie" and "Querube".

Tito Rodríguez is the stage name of the singer, musician and conductor Pablo *Rodríguez Lozada* who was born in Santurce on January 4, 1923, and died in New York on February 28, 1973.

Guitar, vibraphone, maracas and timpani player.

He began his musical activity in 1936.

In his childhood he organized and joined the group Sexteto Nacional, together with  his friend since that time, the musician Mariano Artau and at the age of 13 he joined the "Conjunto Típico Ladí", also called "Conjunto de Industrias Nativas" directed by the musician Ladislao Martínez, with which he recorded together with Rafael Castro, also a member of the group, his first song, the dance "**Amor perdido**", in 1939, recorded by the RCA Victor record label.

Among his best-known boleros are, among others, "Tiemblas", "Inolvidable", "Cuando ya no me quieras", "Que será" and "El que se fue".

He had a sentimental way of interpreting the bolero, although he also sang other popular musical genres such as the mambo, of which he recorded, between 1952 and 1955, six albums with the Tico Records label.

José Feliciano is the stage name of singer, composer and guitarist *José Monserrat Feliciano García*, who was born in Lares on September 10, 1945.

He is considered the first Hispanic American to enter the English-language music market.

He has performed and published more than 600 songs. Its record sales are estimated at 50 million copies.

His composition **"Feliz Navidad"** is one of the most listened to during the Christmas season in the entire world.

He has more than 100 songs recorded, among which are "No hay sombra que me cubra", "Ay, cariño", "La copa rota", "Su hija me gusta", "Paso la vida pensando", "Me has echado al olvido", "Destiny", "Porque te tengo que olvidar", "Come Down Jesus", "Angela", "Rain", "Chico & The Man", "Hard Times In El Barrio" and the instrumentals: "Pegao" and "Affirmation".

He was one of the first artists to include duets in his albums, among which are: "Para decir adiós" with Ann Kelly (1982), "Por ella" with José José, "Un amor así" with Lani Hall, and "Tengo que decirte algo" with Gloria Estefan.

Danny Rivera is the stage name of singer and songwriter *Danny Rivera Méndez*, who was born in Santurce on February 27, 1945.

He began his professional life in 1968 at the San Juan Hotel as a singer of the César Concepción Orchestra, which was the best of its time. That same year he was chosen the Revelation of the Year at a Festival of Popularity and made his recording debut by recording with the group The Clean Cuts "Amor, amor"

Other hits followed, such as "Porque yo te amo", "Fuiste mía un verano", "Manolo", "Mi viejo", "Yo y la rosa" and "Va caiendo una lágrima".

In 1971 he had a huge success with a version of the song "Jesus Christ", by Roberto Carlos, which was followed the following year by the album "Mi hijo", which included two of the most important songs of his career: "Tu pueblo es mi pueblo" and "Amada amante".

In 1980, he signed a contract with the important Venezuelan record label TH and the albums he made there have come to be considered classics, including Alborada, Serenata (which includes an emblematic song of his career, Don Felo's "Madrigal") and Danza para mi pueblo, an album of Puerto Rican dances.

Later he created his own record label.

In addition to bolero, he performs salsa and ballad.

Website: dannyrivera.com

It is known as "**The National Voice of Puerto Rico**."

He has recorded more than seventy albums and "is," reads Wikipedia, the free encyclopedia, "the only Puerto Rican to have performed and sold-out tickets at Carnegie Hall in four different decades (1979, 1989, 1999, 2010).

Among his hits are, among many others, the songs "Madrigal", "Amar o morir", "Mi viejo", "Dos amantes", "Amada amante".

Rafael Muñoz y su Orquesta was one of the many Puerto Rican musical groups that had the bolero as their raw material. The bolero singer **José Luis Moneró**, one of the many soloists who made up that orchestra, belonged to it.

This musician was born in Quebradilla on September 5, 1900, and began his career in an orchestra in his town called Los Cuervos de la Noche. There he was a flute player.

He arrived in San Juan in 1926, where he was part of several orchestras, as he also played the double bass and trumpet.

The source we consulted reveals that in 1932 the El Escambrón Beach club was inaugurated on whose stage the homonymous orchestra was mounted, but its director Don Riverola left taking his place Rafael Muñoz, beginning in 1934 the era of the great orchestra that bore his name and whose repertoire consisted, among other songs, of the boleros "Quiéreme mucho", "Crystal Bells", "Anger", "Words of a Woman" and "My Sweet Sensation" with the unmistakable José Luis Moneró.

Rafael Muñoz died on September 2, 1961.[xlvii]

Los tríos were in the past and still an important tool for the promotion of the bolero.

Among them, Trío Los Fascinantes, Cheito González y su Trío, Armando Vega y su Trío, Trío Éxtasis, Trio Los Tres Nombres, Trío Caribe, Trío Carimari, Los Borincanos, Trío Rafaelito Muñoz, Trío Taboas-Scharon, Trío Borinquen, Trio Los Marcianos, Trío Vegajabeño, Trío Voces de Puerto Rico, Trío Voces de San Juan, Trío Alfa TV. Trío San Juan, Los Tres

Boricuas, Trío Los Cancioneros, Los Hispanos, Los Andinos, Lo Nuevo en Tres y Los Galanes.[xlviii]

GUATEMALA

The presence of the bolero in this Central American country is active, both in composition and in interpretation, which has among its greatest representatives Ricardo Arjona, of international projection, and César de Guatemala, whose best-known work is the bolero "**Mi plegaria**".

César de Guatemala was the stage name of singer-songwriter *César Rodas*, who was born in Chichicastenango on November 1, 1942, and died at the Roosevelt Hospital in Guatemala on December 20, 2018.

He achieved fame in 1974 thanks to the release of the song "**Mi plegaria**", which was very popular in Latin America.

He also composed "A escondidas", "Sufro tu ausencia" and "Sh boom", among many other hits.

Pablo Juárez wrote about his death in the newspaper *Prensa Libre* on December 27, 2018

Singer César de Guatemala, author and interpreter of Mi Plegaria, dies

César Rodas del Valle, better known as César de Guatemala, died at the Roosevelt hospital on Thursday at the age of 76 due to a stroke, according to Otto Escobar, the artist's public relations officer...

... Del Valle had been admitted to the Hermano Pedro Hospital and on December 20 he was transferred to the hospital where he died this Thursday.

"His stroke was on Wednesday and I remember that the next day he spoke very well and was even joking. I told him to behave well and that he had to get his act together because there were many events planned, he replied that he would go to everyone with enthusiasm. Even in his last moments you could tell that he was happy, he was a person who was always characterized by being cheerful and died with a positive attitude," Escobar recalled.

"Cesar was an icon of Guatemalan song, with the song Mi plegaria he obtained a silver record for his sales. He was a person with a lot of humor in the face of adversity. His music was full of simplicity and romanticism. He was a great composer and very jovial in his presentations," said Rebeca Morales, better known as Rebesalsa, singer and president of the Association of Professional Singers of Guatemala.[xlix]

CÉSAR DE GUATEMALA y "MI PLEGARIA" en Amatitlán

On Monday, June 6, 2016, a digital text that can be read in the link http://amatitlanesasi.blogspot.com reported on the first Sunday of that month, the successful national singer "César de Guatemala" who for five decades has performed "Mi Plegaria" performed for the first time at the municipal stadium "Guillermo Slowing", in the mega concert "Unidos por el Hospital", considered one of the best romantic songs of all time and that he has had the pleasure of singing personally in most Latin American countries.

That Sunday he began his show with the song "Amorcito corazón", followed by boleros such as "Reloj", "Gema", and "Perfidia", closing of course with "Mi Plegaria". All pleasantly seasoned with sparks of the good humor that characterizes us chapines.

According to that source, César de Guatemala was "Without a doubt a true winner, a true **"Lord of the song"**. and "One of the first singers from Guatemala to project himself and be recognized internationally".

Una tarde de tríos y boleros

On June 5, 2015, María Mercedes Arce reviewed the Great Trios Concert that took place at the Chamber Theater of the Miguel Ángel Asturias Cultural Center in Guatemala City, within the framework of the XI June Festival.

The Guatemalan trios Nuevo Sol, Los Costello and Los Inseparables de Cobán participated in that event, groups that performed the best of the bolero repertoire, with voices, guitars, requintos and maracas.

Bolero Concert with the National Choir of Guatemala and the Los Príncipes Trio

Another proof of the active presence of the bolero in that country was the concert that took place on Thursday, March 5, 2015, at the Real Palacio de Los Capitanes Cultural Center, Antigua Guatemala.

The event, called **"Le Canta al Amor"**,

His repertoire was the well-known boleros "Bésame mucho", "Amorcito corazón", "Reloj", "Rayito de luna", "Gema", "Sabor a mí" and "Yo soy", among others.

The National Choir of Guatemala, which is a Cultural Heritage of the Nation by Decree 29-93 of 1993, was founded in 1966. Among its constant activities is to offer concerts in various regions of the country, with varied interpretations ranging from the Gregorian style to the Contemporary, with special emphasis on Guatemalan music. Within the choir's repertoire there is also music of all nationalities.

I found no documentation of the Los Príncipes Trio.[1]

Ricardo Arjona is the stage name of guitarist, singer, arranger and author *Édgar Ricardo Arjona Morales*, who was born in Jocotenango on January 19, 1964. He is known as "**El Flaco**" and "**El Trovador de América**".

He has been playing guitar since he was eight years old. He graduated from the School of Communication Science of the University of San Carlos de Guatemala, a profession he never practiced.

At the age of twelve he participated in the 74 Children's Youth Festival contest that he won with the song "**Gracias al mundo**", composed by his father.

By then he composed his first song, "Esa es mi barca".

In his youth he belonged to the basketball clubs Leones de Marte and TRIAS.

In 1988 he traveled to Argentina to participate in the OTI Festival and there he resided, until he went to Mexico and in one of the appointments to get a producer and record his songs one of them, after listening to him, recommended that he dedicate himself to something else.

It is read in Wikipedia, the free encyclopedia, that due to the need to pay the rent where he lived he was forced to write songs for other artists, "Tan solo una mujer" for Bibi Gaytán, and "Detrás de mi ventana" for the album Nueva era de Yuri (1993), which became a hit in 1994, reaching the first position for three weeks on Hot Latin Songs in the United States.

The source adds:

Sony Music, after rejecting it repeatedly, signed it due to a deal arranged by an important producer and friend of the singer-songwriter, consisting of that, if the company wanted to sign two artists for whom it was interested, they had to sign Ricardo as well. After waiting for almost a year after being signed, he decides that it is time to make the album and begins to install everything for production and a week before starting, the company canceled everything and set conditions, because if he wanted to make the album, he had to pay for it himself. He began to record many of his old songs on cassettes and went to publishers to borrow money in exchange for these songs and with that money he recorded his album Animal nocturno. The album is liked, but the company shelved it and did not let anything else happen, until much later Arjona meets Aloysio Reis, the new artistic director of the company, who after being delighted to hear the album, brings it to light and begins the great success as an international singer-songwriter for Ricardo Arjona.

  Among the most successful songs are the titles: "Historia de un taxi", "Señora de las cuatro décadas", "Realmente no estoy tan solo", "Por qué es tan cruel el amor", "Ayúdame Freud", "S:O:S, Rescátame", Quién diría", "Animal nocturno", "Tarde", "Mentiroso", "Pingüinos en la cama", "Dime que no", "Cuando", "Ella y él", "Mujeres" y "Primera vez".

MÉXICO

This country is prodigal in the interpretation and compassion of the bolero and also played an important role in its promotion through 78, 45 and 33 rpm records and through films. There the bolero ranchero subgenre was born.

The first work of this genre dates from 1921. It is **"Morenita mía"** that was born in Yucatán under the authorship of **Armando Villarreal Lozano**, who, in the score, however, did not specify any genre. He was born on August 9, 1903, in San Luis Potosí and died on March 15, 1976.

In addition to this composer, Mexico was the homeland of many others, as well as great performers, such as Agustín Lara, Pedro Infante, Juan Arvizu, Jorge Negrete, María Victoria, Rosiuta Quintana, Juan Gabriel, José Alfredo Jiménez, Ramón Armengod, Luis Aguilar, Tony Aguilar, Alfonso Ortiz Tirado, Consuelo Velásquez, Pedro Vargas, Toña La Negra, Javier Solís, Marco Antonio Muñiz Luis Miguel and many other figures.

Juan Arvizu was the stage name of the performer *Juan Nepomuceno Arvizu Santelices*, who was born in Querétaro on May 22, 1900 and died in Mexico City on November 19, 1985.

He was called **"The Tenor of the Silk Voice"** and his repertoire favored the compositions of Agustín Lara.

He studied music theory and harmony at the National Conservatory of Music.

She began to sing in a children's choir in her hometown.

In 1924 she made her debut at the Teatro Esperanza Iris, in the company of Consuelo Escobar and Ángeles Ottein. Two years later he recorded with the Brunswick label the songs "Varita de nardo" and "Ventanita morada", both by Joaquín Pardavé, but it was RCA Víctor that gave him the opportunity to start a successful career.

The works of Agustín Lara catapulted him to fame.

Agustín Lara, whose full name is *Ángel Agustín María Carlos Fausto Mariano Alfonso Rojas Canela del Sagrado Corazón de Jesús Lara y Aguirre del Pino*, who was  born on October 30, 1900 in Tlacotalpan in the Mexican state of Veracruz and died in Mexico City on November 6, 1970. He was artistically known as "***El Flaco de Oro***", and although he had no academic musical training, his production was prolific.

One of his great works, "Granada", was immortalized by the tenor Mario Lanza. Other great hits of his authorship were, among many others, "Madrid", "La Cumbancha", "Noche de ronda", "Solamente una vez", "Palmera", "María Bonita", "Pecadora", "Revancha", "Coqueta", "Mujeres en mi vida", "Perdida", "La mujer que yo amé". "Palabras de mujer", "Mujer", "Piensa en mí", "Arráncame la vida", "Veracruz", "Cada noche un amor", "Como dos puñales", "Pervertida", "El farolito", "Cuerdas de mi guitarra", "Humo en los ojos", "Imposible" and "Santa".

In addition to boleros, he composed pasodobles, tangos, ballads and pasacalles, among other genres.

Pedro Vargas was the stage name of singer, actor and composer *Pedro Cruz Mata*, who was born on April 29, 1906 in San Miguel Allende and died in Mexico City on October 30, 1989.

He was known as **"The Nightingale of the Americas"**, **"The Continental Tenor"** and **"The Samurai of Song"**.

As an actor, he was part of the Golden Age of Mexican Cinema and participated in more than 70 films.

On his first visit to Buenos Aires, he recorded two songs of his own for the RCA Victor label: "Porteñita mía" and "Me fui".

He was one of the best and most successful interpreters of the composer Agustín Lara, with an extensive repertoire that included lyrical themes such as "Jinetes en el Cielo", ranchera songs such as "Allá en el Rancho Grande", boleros such as "Obsesión", sung in two voices with Benny Moré; and nostalgic songs such as "Alfonsina and the sea".

Toña La Negra was the stage name of the singer and actress *Antonia del Carmen Peregrino Álvarez,* who was born in Veracruz on November 2, 1912, and died in Mexico City on November 19, 1982.

She was called **"The Jarocha Sensation"**.

She was active from 1932 to 1982.

Part of her artistic fame came from the admirable interpretation he made of the boleros and other tropical songs of the composer Agustín Lara. She was performing one of her boleros, **"Enamorada"**, she met Emilio Azcárraga Vidaurreta who, together with Enrique Contel, baptized her as Toña La Negra.

Agustín Lara composed for her, among others, the songs "Lamento Jarocho", "Veracruz", "Noche criolla", "Oración Caribe", "Palmera", "La clave azul" and "La cumbancha", which they presented together in a musical revue at the Teatro Esperanza, in December 1932, with such success that they had to prolong their presentations for a long time.

She was part of the cast of the XEW radio station, where she appeared sometimes accompanied by Lara and sometimes by the Alfredo Girón orchestra.

She recorded for the RCA Victor label, being "El cacahuatero", one of the first recordings.

María Victoria is the stage name used by the singer and actress María *Victoria Cervantes*, who was born in Guadalajara, Jalisco on February 26, 1933.

She entered the digital market at the end of 2013, launching his collection "The music of my films".

Among his singles are "Mucho, mucho, mucho", "Que bonito siento", "Venganza", "Mil besos", "Que divino" and "Cuidadito".

She recorded more than 500 songs, which have been compiled in around 100 albums, among which the song **"Estoy tan enamorada"** stands out.

She inspired songs by Juan Gabriel and Agustín Lara.

She won several Gold Records, Palme d'Or and Heralds.

Her performance in the cinema was copious.

Consuelo Velásquez was a composer and pianist who was born in Ciudad Guzmán on August 21, 1916, and died in Mexico City on January 22, 2005.

At a very young age, at 19, the bolero **"Bésame mucho"** catapulted her to fame, although when she wrote it, she did not know what a kiss was. He was also authored, among others, by the titles "Amar y vivir", "Franqueza", "Que seas feliz" and "Verdad amarga".

"**Bésame mucho**" has been considered the most important bolero of the twentieth century. Written in 1940, the first to record was Emilio Tuero. and over time, it was passed from one artist to another with different adaptations, with Pedro Infante's version being one of the best known, as well as an English version by The Beatles.

Pedro Infante was a film actor and singer who was born in Mazatlán, Sinaloa, on November 18, 1917, and died in Mérida, Yucatán, on April 15, 1957.

From 1939 he appeared in more than 60 films, and from 1943 he recorded approximately 310 songs.

He played various musical instruments. and was the vocalist of several orchestras.

His first musical recording, "**El Soldado Raso**" was made on November 19, 1943, for the Peerless Records label, although other sources say that the first song, he recorded was the waltz Mañana, which passed without pain or glory.

Among the most successful boleros he performed are "Bésame mucho", "Te quiero así", "La que se fue", "Ella", "Cien años", and "Amorcito corazón".

José Alfredo Jiménez (January 19, 1926 – November 23, 1973) was *a Mexican singer, actor and composer who died in Dolores, Hidalgo.*

At the age of 14 he composed his first songs.

In 1948 he sang for the first time on XEX and a few months later he managed to sing on the famous XEW station, accompanied by the trio Los Rebeldes.

The definitive triumph was achieved in 1950, the year in which Andrés Huesca and his Costeños recorded their song entitled "Yo", a musical piece that quickly became the first of a long series of hits.

His musical production includes, among many others, the songs: "El rey", "No me amenaces", "Amanecí en tus brazos", "Paloma querida", "Camino de Guanajuato", "Cuando vivas conmigo", "Corazón", "Te solté la rienda", "Caballo blanco", "Pa' todo el año", "Cuando sale la luna", "¡Qué bonito amor!", "Un mundo raro" and "La enorme distancia".

He won more than 100 awards in recognition of his work as a composer and singer, including 16 Gold Records.

Joaquín Pardavé was a film, theater and television actor, film director, screenwriter and composer who was born in Pénjamo, Guanajuato, on September 30, 1900, and died in Mexico City on July 20, 1955.

As a telegraph operator for the National Railways of Mexico at the Paredón station, he composed the piece "**Carmen**", dedicated to Carmen Delgado.

He composed the music for the film "México se derrumba" and, in collaboration with José Palacios Montalvo and "El fracaso del sábado".

He gave life to 120 compositions, among them, "Negra consentida", "Falsa", "No hagas llorar a esa mujer", "Ventanita morada", "La Panchita", "Aburr me voy", "Caminito de la sierra", "Varita de nardo", "Bésame en la boca", or "Porque lloran tus ojos", a work that in general covered a total of 120 compositions.

Alfonso Ortiz Tirado was a prominent Mexican tenor singer and orthopedist, who was born in Álamos, Sonora, on January 24, 1893, and died in Mexico City on September 7, 1960.

As a doctor, he treated personalities such as the painter **Frida Kahlo** and the composer **Agustín Lara**, who underwent surgery on the cheek.

As a singer. he toured Central and South America, the United States and some European countries giving recitals, without neglecting the practice of medicine.

He acted in the film "La última canción" (1933) alongside the actress María Luisa Zea.

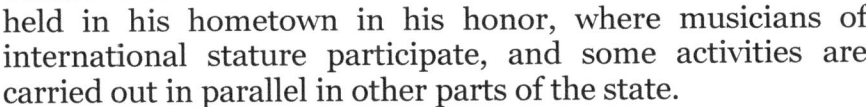

Since 1984, the Alfonso Ortiz Tirado International Festival has been held in his hometown in his honor, where musicians of international stature participate, and some activities are carried out in parallel in other parts of the state.

His repertoire was made up, among other songs, of "Clavel de aire", "Oración Caribe", "Llora campana llora", "Por si no te vuelvo a ver", "Muñequita linda", "Amapola", "Pregón de las flores", "Palmera", "Peregrino de amor", "Lamento borincano" and "Lamento gitano".

Juan Gabriel was the stage name of composer, singer, record producer and philanthropist *Alberto Aguilera Valadez*, who was born on January 7, 1950 in Parácuaro, Michoacán, and died on August 28, 2016 in Santa Monica, California, United States.

He was called "***The Divo of America***".

He sold more than 100 million records as a solo artist and his compositions were translated into Turkish, German, French, Italian, Tagalog, Japanese, Greek, Papiamento, Portuguese and English.

The first stage of his successful career began on August 4, 1971, when he changed the stage name **Adán Luna** to **Juan Gabriel**.

Among the songs of his authorship successfully performed by Rocío Dúrcal are "Siempre en mi mente", "Juro que nunca volveré", "Amor eterno", "El Noa-Noa", "Inocente, pobre amigo", "La diferencia", "Mi fracaso", "Buenos días, señor Sol", "En esta primavera", "La muerte del palomo" and "Ya para qué".

Their songs were also performed, among many others, by Lucha Villa, Raphael, Vicente Fernández, Lupita D'Alessio, María Victoria, Pedro Vargas, Lola Beltrán, Amalia Mendoza and Cornelio Reyna.

Ana Gabriel is the stage name of singer and songwriter *María Guadalupe Araujo Yong*, who was born on December 10, 1955 in Guamúchil.

Since I was 9 years old I have been inclined towards music and composition.

She never studied singing or vocalization.

She began her artistic career on September 15, 1974, in Tijuana, led by José Barrientos, her manager at the time, who made her known as Ana Gabriel.

In 1985 he recorded his first full-length album entitled "Un estilo" and the following year he managed to participate in the OTI Festival, reaching fifth place with the song "A tu lado" that he included in the album Sagitario, where there are also songs such as "Y Aquí Estoy", "Eso no Basta" and "Mar y Arena".

Three years later he managed to position himself internationally, within the U.S. market, with his album Tierra de Nadie that remained on the Billboard charts for several months.

Among his distinctions is the Diamond Record award for having sold more than one million records in Chile.

He has recorded a duet with artists such as Armando Manzanero, Pedro Fernández, Yuri, Plácido Domingo, Jon Secada, Rocío Jurado, Vikki Carr and José Feliciano, among others.

Javier Solís was the stage name adopted by singer *Gabriel Siria Levario*, who was born in Nogales, Sonora, September 1, 1931 – died in Mexico City on April 19, 1966.

He was known as **"The King of Bolero Ranchero"**

Initially he sang tangos in public places of shows known as carpa.

He began a new stage performing in restaurants and as part first of the Guadalajara Duo and then of the Flamingo Trio, later called Trio Mexico,

Around 1950 he recorded his first creations made up of the songs "Punto negro", "Tómate esa copa", "Virgen de barro" and "Te voy a dar mi corazón", produced with the Los Galantes Trio.

The stage name of Javier Solís was suggested by his friend Manuel Garay.

His incomplete discography includes the albums "Javier Solís", "Canta Javier", "Añoranzas", "Hits de Javier Solís", "Boleros, Boleros, Boleros", "Prisionero del mar", "Romance", "Lara, Grever, Baena", "Romance", "Sombras" and "Payaso".

María Grever was the stage name adopted by the singer and composer *María Joaquina de la Portilla Torres*, who was born on September 14, 1885, in León, Guanajuato, and died in New York, United States, on December 15, 1951.

She composed concerts and concert music and more than 800 popular songs, mostly boleros.

In the early 1920s she devoted herself to singing and recorded two albums in the United States. She also worked as a music scorer for several films for Paramount and 20th Century Fox.

Around that time – it is read in Wikipedia, the free encyclopedia – he began to compose songs, but his first great success came when the Mexican tenor José Mojica recorded his song "Júrame", thus becoming its first performer. Her songs have been recorded by great performers such as: Enrico Caruso, Ray Conniff, Bobby Darin, Nicolás Urcelay, Andy Russell, Dinah Washington, Libertad Lamarque, Dean Martin, Aretha Franklin, Rod Stewart, Plácido Domingo, Alfonso Ortiz Tirado, Juan Arvizu, Nestor Mesta Chayres, Barry Manilow, Natalie Cole, Gloria Estefan, Amy Winehouse, Luis Miguel, John Serry Sr. and Javier Solís, among others.

In addition to "Jurame", the songs "Todo Mi Ser", "Así", "Cuando volver a tu lado", "Te quiero, dijiste", "Por si no te vuelvo a ver", "Volveré", "Despedida", "Cuando me vaya" and "Tipitin", among many others, are also known.

Néstor Chayres was the stage name adopted by the film actor and singer *Néstor Mesta Cháyres*, who was born in Ciudad Lerdo, on February 26, 1908, and died in Mexico City, June 29, 1971.

He was known as "**The Gypsy of Mexico**".

He began his professional career in 1929 performing songs by Jorge del Moral and Agustín Lara.

His repertoire of popular music, among other songs, included "Noche de ronda", "La morena de mi copla", "Arráncame la vida!", "El relicario", "Farolito", "Oración Caribe", "Princesita", "Pregón de las flores", "Mi pobre reja", "Somos diferentes", "Asturiana", "La panda", "Clavelitos", "Mi maja", "Granada", "Hoy no quiero vivir", "No espera nada de ti", "Noche de mar", "Mucho más", "Manolete", "Silverio", "No te vayas", "Todo mi ser", "Te espero", "Tus lindos ojos", "La vida castiga", "Porque te quiero", "Alma mía", "Cuando vuelve a tu lado" and "Paso a paso".

Guty Cárdenas was the stage name used by the singer, guitarist and composer *Augusto Alejandro Cárdenas Pinelo*, who was born in Mérida, Yucatán, on December 12, 1905, and died in Mexico City on April 5, 1932.

She made her singing debut at an anniversary event of the newspaper *Excelsior and in the contest* "La fiesta de la canción" with her composition "Nunca", whose lyrics had been written by Ricardo López Méndez.

From this moment on, he made solo presentations and signed a contract with the Mexican record label Huici, which would later become Discos Peerless. In that company he made his first recordings, including the song "Nunca". Then, he became part of the exclusive artists of the Columbia Records company.

Among his best-known compositions are "Caminante del Mayab", with lyrics by Antonio Mediz Bolio; "Flor", inspired by the poem of the same name by the Venezuelan poet Pérez Bonalde, considered by some to be the first bolero in Venezuela; "Un rayito de sol", "Fondo azul", "Golondrina viajera", "Para olvidarte", "Peregrino de amor" and "Ojos tristes".

Chucho Martínez Gil was the stage name used by the singer and composer *Jesús Bojalil Gil*, who was born on December 19, 1917, in Puebla de Zaragoza, and died on May 22, 1988

He began his musical career in 1934, on a concert tour with Gonzalo Curiel.

His first hits were the waltz "Ensoñación" and "Dos arbolitos", a song that was also performed by several singers outside of Mexico.

Other important works were "Río cristal", "Mañana vendrás", "Rosita se está bañando", "Te vi llegar", "Un recuerdo", "Mi Magdalena", "El pocito de Nacaquinia", "Llegó el amor", "Esclavo", "Pimpollo", "A bailar Cha", "Terroncito terroncito", "Me duele el corazón", "Cinco letras que lloran", "Menos que nada", "El naranjo", "Te seguiré", "Ya me voy lejos", "Saudades Do Brasil", "The Scapular" and "The Flower". Some of his works were composed together with his cousins Pablo and Carlos Martínez Gil.

The bolero "Mi Magdalena" was popularized by the Los Panchos Trio.

Marco Antonio Muñiz was a singer and actor who was born in Guadalajara, Jalisco, on March 3, 1933. He is known as: "***The Ambassador of Romanticism***" and "***The Luxury of Mexico***".

Before becoming famous, she sang in the choir of a church in her hometown and was part of several musical groups.

In 1959 he began his career as a soloist with the songs "Luz y Sombra" and "Escándalo".

In 1965, already as a recognized and consolidated soloist, he began one tour after another that would take him to the most important stages in Latin America, the United States and Spain; reaping hits such as: "Adelante", "Compréndeme", "Capullito de Alhelí" and "Por Amor", among many others.

That year he was in Venezuela and made contact with typical Venezuelan music, recording the bolero-passage. "La noche de tu partida", "Suerte" and "Venezuela en la música de Juan Vicente Torrealba".

He returned to that country in 1969 and recorded the album "Serenata en Venezuela".

His most successful albums are, among others, "Marco Antonio Muñiz with Los Trovadores Caribe", "Corazón maldito", "Mi novia es Guadalajara", "Marco Antonio Muñiz" – "La serenata del siglo, with La Rondalla Tapatía. He performs Gonzalo Curiel and Gabriel Ruiz Galindo, "Salsa, la manera de Marco Antonio" (his foray into tropical music), "Mi Borinquen querido, un homenaje a la música autoctona puertorriqueña", "Homenaje a Pedro Infante" and "Homenaje a José Alfredo Jiménez".

Vicente Fernández is a singer, actor and record producer who was born on February 17, 1940 in Guadalajara.

He is known as "**El charro de Huentitán**", "**El Hijo del Pueblo**" and "**El Rey**".

He began his professional career in 1964 and in the course of it has won two Grammy Awards, eight Latin

Grammy Awards, fourteen Lo Nuestro Awards and a star on the Hollywood Walk of Fame.

In April 2010 it reached the figure of 75 million copies sold worldwide.

In 1972 his worldwide hit and ranchero anthem, **"Volver, Volver"**, consolidated him as one of the greatest ranchero singers of all time. With this song she broke all sales records in Latin America, Spain and the United States.

Other of his hits were the songs "Para siempre", "Las llaves de mi alma", "Que te vaya bonito", "El Arracadas", "Por tu maldito amor", "Aunque me duela el alma", "Mujeres divinas" and "Me voy a quitar de en medio" and many more.

On September 25, 2007, he released his album "Para siempre", certified as a Diamond and Gold Record in Mexico; while in the United States it reached its sixth Platinum Record just weeks after its release.

On April 16, 2016, he performed his last farewell concert at the Azteca stadium, he sang around 45 songs, but announced that, although it was his last concert, he was not retiring from music.

Antonio Aguilar was the stage name used by singer, producer and screenwriter *José Pascual Antonio Aguilar Márquez Barraza*, who was born in Villanueva, Zacatecas, on May 17, 1919 and died in Mexico City on June 19, 2007.

He was known as **"El Charro de México"**

In 2000 he won the Prize Lo Nuestro for Excellence and four years later he received the Latin Grammy Award for Musical Excellence.

His discography surpassed 160 albums with sales of more than 25 million copies.

He has a star on the Hollywood Walk of Fame.

His bolero career began at XEW.

He produced, among many others, the albums "Tres Días", "Vivo en México", "Amor del alma", "Joyas", "Peregrina", "15 Éxitos con tambora", "15 Éxitos con banda", "Toda mi vida" and "Frente a frente".

Gabriel Ruiz Galindo was a musician and composer who was born in Guadalajara on March 18, 2018, and died in Mexico City on January 31, 1999.

He was among the founding members of the Society of Authors and Composers of Mexico.

In his hometown he began his musical studies that he concluded at the National Conservatory of Music, as a violinist.

He composed more than 400 songs, the most popular being the boleros: "Amor, amor", "Desperately", "Mar" and "Usted". The first three were co-authored with the poet Ricardo López Méndez and the last with José Antonio Zorrilla Martínez.

His bolero "Condition" was popularized by Chucho Avellanet and "Despierta" was popularized by Pedro Infante.

Another bolero of his authorship, "**El vicio**", was made known by Marco Antonio Muñiz.

Manuel Esperón was a musician and composer who was born in Mexico City on August 3, 1911 and died in Cuernavaca, Morelos, on February 13, 2011.

He was president for life of the Society of Authors and Composers of Mexico, musical director of almost 500 films and artistic director of several radio stations.

He composed more than 900 songs, including the famous bolero "Flor de azalea", "Noche Plateada", "Tequila con Limón", "El día que me quieras", "Carta de Amor", "Traigo un Amor", "Dulce patria", "Fiesta mexicana", "Que te cuesta", "Amor con amor se paga", "Although they want it or not", "Amorcito corazón", "Y dicen por ahí" and "El sueño".

Manuel Esperón's songs inspired romanticism in Mexico

On Monday, February 14, 2011, on the occasion of his death the day before, José Luis Blancarte, of Ciudadanía Express, wrote the report that is transcribed below:

Conaculta **Oaxaca, Mexico**. - *He was the greatest composer that Mexican cinema has had. Composer Manuel Esperón González (Mexico City, August 3, 1911 – Cuernavaca, Morelos, February 13, 2011) died yesterday, leaving behind a vast body of songs, waltzes and vernacular pieces that inspired the dreams of Mexicans for decades. His prolific work was developed in the disco, radio and television industry, but preponderantly in cinematography, where he came to score more than 500 films, especially from the so-called Golden Age of national cinema. For the same reason, Esperón was highly appreciated by figures of the big screen such as Pedro Infante, María Félix, Jorge Negrete, Dolores del Río and Pedro Armendáriz. One of the first films for which he wrote music was La mujer del puerto, starring Andrea Palma. Some of the actresses and actors with whom he became friends were Elsa Aguirre, María Elena Marqués, Silvia Pinal, María Antonieta Pons, Irma Dorantes, Cantinflas, Joaquín Pardavé and Vicente Fernández, for whom he made one of his last works by scoring a film. From a very young age he was characterized by wearing a beret, and always willing to improvise a new song on the piano, but* *he also stood out as a brilliant arranger, in the line of the Mexican school, which put forward the melody of the vast Mexican popular heritage. Music critic Juan Arturo Brenan, in an interview with La Jornada, commented that he thinks that "it would be possible to trace a partial history, let's say, a minimal history of a certain era of Mexican cinema through the music and songs that he wrote for our cinematography." The lyrics of Esperón's more than 900 songs, such as Amorcito corazón; Mine; I will not return or ¡Ay Jalisco no te rajes!, were written by composers such as Ernesto Cortázar or Pedro de Urdimalas (Jesús Camacho Villaseñor), among their most notable lyricists, also Ricardo El Vate López Méndez, Felipe Bermejo and Zacarías Gómez Urquiza, among other important authors, who were interpreted by voices of the stature of Pedro Vargas, Toña La Negra, Pedro Infante or Jorge Negrete. Singers of the stature of Libertad Lamarque, Antonio Aguilar, Luis Aguilar, Javier Solís, Tin Tan and Alberto Vázquez, among many others. Among the hundreds of films for which he composed music are: I danced with Don Porfirio; I have to eat that prickly pear; The woman of the port; The three Garcias; The abandoned ones; Great casino; We the poor; You rich people; Oh Jalisco, don't give up!; Love is repaid with love; A Love Letter and For Your Damn Love. Manuel Esperón, grandson of the Oaxacan composer Macedonio Alcalá, began in music from a very young age, encouraged by his mother Raquel González Cantú, who was a concert pianist. He was also a cousin-brother of maestro Ignacio Fernández Esperón, known as Tata Nacho. In adolescence he studied technical studies at the Polytechnic (ESIME), he was also interested in the plastic arts at the Academy of San Carlos, but his fingers were hardened to play the piano, so he decided to enter the Popular School of Music, which would become the National School of Fine Arts, because he was interested in having a formal base to dedicate himself fully to composition and musical arrangement. In the biography of maestro Esperón, published on the website of the Society of Authors and Composers of Mexico (SACM) states that, before venturing into cinema, Esperón "belonged to the artistic caravan of the Soler Brothers. With them he toured part of southeastern Mexico and Central and South America." In those adventures, "he had to see the first sound film; it was The Jazz Singer, with Al Johnson." It was 1929... His dream would be fulfilled in 1933. At the age of 22, she wrote her first song professionally for a film, The Woman of the Port. He composed the theme song with lyrics by El Vate Ricardo López Méndez. He also composed some parts of the background music. He also contributed to the Hollywood film industry. He worked for Metro Golden Mayer, Paramount and Disney. In the latter he collaborated with Walt Disney in the film Los Tres Caballeros, for which he made all the Mexican part. Esperón introduced mariachi to the cinema, the semblance of the SACM abounds, and sought that the lyrical performers study music; In this way, the composer managed to couple the orchestra with the mariachi for the instrumental arrangements of the films. Throughout more than seventy years of artistic career, many figures in the music industry have performed Esperón's songs, such as Yuri, Eugenia León, Thalía, Tania Libertad, Aída Cuevas, Alberto Vázquez, Julio Iglesias, Plácido Domingo, Vicente Fernández and Luis Miguel, to mention just a few. He also created symphonic arrangements of Mexican popular music, of his own most important songs and of other Mexican composers, such as Guty Cárdenas, Ricardo Palmerín, Pepe Guízar, José Alfredo Jiménez, Alfredo Carrasco and Agustín Lara, among others.*

Numerous concerts have been presented with the music of maestro Esperón and his rhapsody entitled México 1910 was premiered internationally, which contains Mexican music of the Revolution, developed at an orchestral and choral level. Another of his most outstanding works is the arrangement of the Classical Waltzes of Romantic

Mexico, for symphony orchestra, mixed choir of one hundred voices and coloratura soprano; presented in a series of these concerts under the baton of the famous conductor Sergio Cárdenas, in the Nezahualcóyotl Hall and various cities in the interior of the Republic. For several years, Esperón belonged to the Board of Directors of the SACM, which has been chaired by composers such as Roberto Cantoral and Armando Manzanero. Among the recognitions received by Manuel Esperón, in 1941, are the RCA Gold Medal; Ariel for the music of the film *Cantaclaro*, 1945; Ariel for the music of the film *Cuando me vaya,* based on the life of María Grever, 1953; Gold Medal Gonzalo Curiel, 1958; Quetzalcoatl Medal, 1983; Ignacio Toscano Medal of Cinematographic Merit, 1984; Gold Medal of the Society of Authors and Composers of Mexico; Silver Goddess Pecime, 1990; National Prize for Sciences and Arts, 1990.

VENEZUELA

This country has made great contributions to the history of bolero both in composition and in interpretation. Every July 2, in memory of the date of Felipe **Pirela's death**, the National Bolero Day is celebrated.

The musician and composer **Lorenzo Herrera** is credited with incorporating, from the radio, that musical genre that has so enriched popular culture.

From its composers have emerged, among many others, the universal boleros "Desesperanza", by María Luisa Escobar; "Motivos", by Ítalo Pizzolante; "Write to Me", by Guillermo Castillo Bustamante and "Consented Life", by Homero Parra.

The history of Venezuelan bolero music records the names of Felipe Pirela, Alfredo Sadel, José Luis Rodríguez, Mirla Castellanos, Mayra Martí, Eduardo Lanz, Marco Tulio Maristany, Graciela Naranjo, Mirla Castellanos, Elisa Soteldo, Canelita Medina, Rafa Galindo, Vladimir Lozano, Corina Peña, Nohemy Berlatti, Nelson Henriquez, Lorenzo González, Enrique Rivas, Mario Suárez, Oswaldo Morales. Simón Díaz, Neyda Perdomo, Óscar D'León, Lila Morillo, Rudy Márquez, Esperanza Márquez, Henry Stephen, Floria Márquez, Trino Mora, Rosalinda García, Toña Granado, Joel Urdaneta, Raúl Naranjo, Mirtha Pérez, Nancy Ramos, Delia, Marlene, Raquel Castaño, Luisín Landáez, Gerardo Valentino, Nancy Toro, Mirna Ríos, Héctor Cabrera, Héctor Murga, Josué Hernández, Devorah Sasha, Estelita del Llano, Rosa Virginia Chacín, María Teresa Chacín, Conny Méndez, Simón Díaz, Josué Hernández and Pecos Kanvas, among many others less known of the new generations.

Lorenzo Herrera was the artistic name of the composer *Lorenzo Esteban Herrera Markfoy*, who is credited with the introduction of the bolero into the Venezuelan musical heritage through the radio. He was among the pioneers of the dissemination of Venezuelan music abroad

He was born in Caracas on August 2, 1896 and died in the same city on January 21, 1960.

He was known as the composer of the 500 hits, since he composed more than five hundred songs, most of which were resounding hits in his time, in the genres merengue, guasa, boleros and pasodobles.

He recorded with the RCA Victor and Columbia Records labels.

In New York he composed many of his works, among others the famous pasodoble "La Sultana del Ávila". He also composed the songs "Luisa", "Josefina", "Rosalinda", "El Bachaco", "Mi Rancho", "La Mula Rucia", "Canta Ruiseñor", "El Primer Amor", "Ya no sufras corazón", "Vente pa´ca mi negra", "Caminito del llano adentro", "El Petróleo" "El Coletón", "Chupa tu Mamey" and "Compae Pancho", which has been used as a starting point for the teaching of the Venezuelan cuatro.

Alfredo Sadel was the stage name used by the composer, film actor and lyrical and popular singer *Alfredo Sánchez*, who was born in Caracas on February 22, 1930 and died in the same city on June 28, 1989.

He was known as **"*Venezuela's favorite tenor*"** and is considered by many musicologists as the most important popular and lyrical performer in Venezuelan musical history.

His artistic vocation was manifested from a young age and he participated in the choir of the Domingo Savio School of Los Teques, where Father Calderón and Father Sidi contributed to give him musical instruction and scenic art. He also had drawing and painting skills and his caricatures were published in the newspaper *La Esfera* and the humorous magazine *Fantoches*.

Their first presentation was at the Cathedral of Caracas. There she sang the Ave Maria and successfully impressed the public and was fortunate to find patrons who helped her to train academically at the Superior School of Music of Caracas and continued throughout her life in Mexico City, New York, Buenos Aires, Barcelona, Salzburg and Milan.

With the income as a cartoonist in an advertising agency, he paid for the recording of his first 78 RPM album, with the songs: the bolero "Desesperación" and the pasodoble "El Diamante Negro", as a tribute to the bullfighter Luis Sánchez, nicknamed as such.

Her voice internationalized the bolero **"Desesperanza"**, by María Luisa Escobar.

Elisa Soteldo was a composer and singer who was born in Barquisimeto, Lara State, on July 25, 1922, and died in Miami, United States, on January 22, 2016.

She sang in English, Italian, Portuguese and French

Musical training in theory, music theory and singing was obtained from his father, Professor Rafael Soteldo; and piano, with his mother, Professor Ángela Soteldo, and Professor Blanca Estrella Méscoli.

In her hometown, as a young man, he participated in choirs under the direction of his father, performing pontifical masses and sacred music for the celebration of Holy Week.

She became the first woman member of an orchestra, that of Luís Alfonzo Larraín, in 1941.

In 1967 he founded Las Voces Blancas de Elisa Soteldo, a school of music, singing and acting; awarded at festivals in Italy, Denmark and Turkey, nursery of many interpreters of bolero and other popular musical genres.

The musician and orchestra director, Aldemaro Romero composed the song Mi melancolía, which was his favorite song.

She was the producer of the musical comedy "Annie" (Anita, The Little Orphan), under the artistic direction of Horacio Peterson, with an orchestra conducted by Chuchito Sanoja; of the Nutcracker and Memories of Mama Blanca.[li]

Mirla Castellanos is the stage name used by singer, actress, composer, broadcaster and presenter *Mirla Josefina Castellanos Peñaloza*, who was born in Valencia, Carabobo State, on March 31, 1941.

She is known as **"La Primerísima"** and **"La Primerísima de América"**

She has been one of the most successful and recognized Spanish-speaking singers in recent decades, being the only one in the history of Venezuela, so far, who has won the prestigious Billboard award, which she won for her album "Vuelve Pronto", in addition to having obtained a variety of recognitions and having shared the stage with great artists nationally and internationally. He has obtained a series of triumphs in important festivals, including the Benidorm Festival in Spain, Onda Nueva in Caracas, the OTI Music Festival in Mexico, the Mallorca Festival and the Greece Festival among others.

Her artistic memorial includes, among others, the successful interpretation of the songs "El abuelo", "Vuelve pronto", "Si no estás tu", Mientras te olvido "Muera el amor",

"La vida es una tómbola", "Día y noche", "Mi próximo amor", "Porque el amor se va", "Di que no soy yo", "No le hagas lo que a mí", "La noche de Chicago", "Sr. juez" and "Maldito amor", of which he sold more than 500,000 copies.

She has been among the pioneers of Venezuela's musical internationalization since 1961, with a record of more than 13 million copies of her albums sold.

Graciela Naranjo was a singer and actress who was born in Maiquetía, Vargas State, on December 25, 1916, and died in Caracas on April 11, 2001.

She was a pioneer, in Venezuela, of radio, cinema and television.

In 1931 she made her professional debut as a bolero singer. She appeared in movies and had his own TV show.

From the mid-1930s to the late 1940s, he shared the stage with many prestigious artists from Venezuela and around the world, including Ary Barroso, Bobby Capó, Celia Cruz, Wilfredo Fernández, Carlos Gardel, Tito Guízar, Agustín Lara, Alfonzo Ortiz Tirado, the Trío Matamoros, Pedro Vargas and the Cuban Vieja Trova Santiaguera, among many others.

She sang music by various composers, such as the Mexican Agustín Lara, and the Puerto Ricans Pedro Flores and Rafael Hernández Marín.

Conny Méndez was the stage name used by singer, actress and composer *Juana María de la Concepción Méndez Guzmán*, who was born in Caracas on April 11, 1898, and died in Miami, United States, on November 26, 1979.

The Bolero in Latin America

In 1946 she founded the Christian Metaphysics Movement of Venezuela, disseminator of the teachings of the Count of Saint Germain.

She composed more than forty musical works. but the best known were "Venezuela habla cantando" and "La negrita Marisol". Other of his compositions are the songs "Mi alma y yo", "Déjame", "La transformación", "Mal de ojo", "Ranchito", "Tierruca", La plata", "Fruto mestizo", "Allí" and "Macumba".

She toured internationally offering singing and guitar concerts

Rafa Galindo was the stage name of singer *Rafael Ernesto Galindo Oramas*, who was born in La Victoria, Aragua State, on October 24, 1921, and died in Caracas on May 25, 2010.

He was active from 1940 to 2010.

He was called "***The Nightingale of the Radio***", and "The ***Troubadour of the Radio***".

He initially worked with the "Trio Antillano" and then became part of the "Orquesta de los Hermanos Rivas".

From this group, at the age of eighteen, he joined the "Venezuelan Boys Orchestra" and then was hired by the Billo's Caracas Boys orchestra in which he remained until 1946, when he had managed to achieve prestige in the listening public.

From this initial period are the boleros "Ven", original by Manuel Sánchez Acosta, "Noche de mar", by José Reina and "La cita", by Freddy Coronado.

Rosalinda García was the stage name of singer *Rosalinda García Wusthrons*, who was born in Caracas on April 17, 1946, and died in the same city on March 5, 1998.

Despite being a lyrical singer, she also performed boleros and Venezuelan music.

Among many other popular hits, the songs "Hastío" and "Damisela encantadora", by Ernesto Lecuona; "Alma mía" and "Cuando me vaya", by María Grever, "Solamente una vez", "Azul" and "Farolito", by Agustín Lara; "Silencio" and "Noche y día", by Rafael Hernández; "Flores de Galipán", by Juan Avilán; "Panama viejo", by Ricardo Fábrega, "Naranjas de Valencia", by María Luisa Escobar, and "Voraz", a compilation by maestro Vicente Emilio Sojo.

She recorded the albums: "Cantares de Venezuela"; "Concierto de Amor", "Clásicos Venezolanos", volúmenes I, II y III; "Perfil Romántico" y "La Reina", etc.[lii]

Eduardo Lanz was a singer who was born in Caracas on August 31, 1984, At the beginning of his professional career he felt a preference for lyrical songs, but as the field of action was very restricted, he chose to dedicate himself to popular singing. His first name was *Eduardo Lanz Rodríguez*.

In 1942 he performed for several months in Medellín, Colombia, and then recorded in Bogotá with the José María Tena orchestra.

At a medical congress in Caracas, Alfonso Ortiz Tirado met him and proposed to hire him to accompany him on his tours and share his contracts with him. And he accompanied him for two years in Argentina, where in 1945 he recorded several successful boleros with the orchestra led by Víctor S. Lister, including "Estás en mí", "Nunca mientas", "Compréndeme" and others. He also traveled to Cuba and Mexico with great success. In Mexico he was part of the cast of the film "Voces de Primavera" with Adalberto Martínez "Resortes" and in that film Lanz sang "Amanecer", by José Reina, which he had already recorded with two voices with Ortiz Tirado in Venezuela. He was the first interpreter of "Desesperanza", by María Luisa Escobar.

Guillermo Castillo Bustamante was a musician and composer who was born in Caracas on June 25, 1910, and died in the same city on October 6, 1974.

He composed more than three hundred songs, mainly boleros, one of the most famous, "Escríbeme", he wrote in the prison of Ciudad Bolívar when he was a political prisoner of the dictatorship of General Marcos Pérez Jiménez.

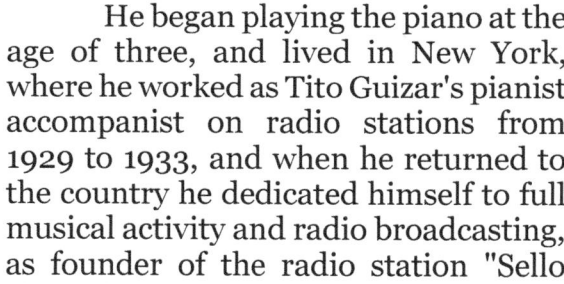

He began playing the piano at the age of three, and lived in New York, where he worked as Tito Guizar's pianist accompanist on radio stations from 1929 to 1933, and when he returned to the country he dedicated himself to full musical activity and radio broadcasting, as founder of the radio station "Sello Rojo" that would later be called "Radiodifusora Venezuela".

On May 22, 1937, he founded the first modern orchestra in the country, the "Swing Time", and in Havana, as an exile, he joined the "Septeto Habanero" in 1949.

He made jazz duets with Antonio Lauro, the consecrated Venezuelan composer of academic music, and created piano solos for Pedro Vargas and María Antonieta Pons.

The bolero "Escríbeme" had Alfredo Sadel as its first performer, who made it known in Víctor Saume's television program, "El Show de las Doce", which was broadcast on Radio Caracas Television.

In addition to Alfredo Sadel he was later interpreted, among many others, by Lucho Gatica, Javier Solís, "Los Cuatro Hermanos Silva", Rosita Quintana, Alfonso Ortiz Tirado, Roberto Yanez and Simón Díaz.[liii]

María Luisa Escobar was the stage name adopted by the pianist, violinist and lyrical singer *María Luisa González Gragirena*, who was born in Valencia, Carabobo State, on December 5, 1898, and died in Caracas on May 14, 1985.

She was among the founders of the Ateneo de Caracas, the Ateneo de Valencia and the Venezuelan Association of Authors and Composers.

She wrote numerous songs, ballads, Venezuelan regional airs, operettas and musical dramas, but her best-known work was the bolero "**Desesperanza**", which was first performed by the Venezuelan baritone Eduardo Lanz, recorded and popularized internationally by Alfredo Sadel and selected as Song of the Year in Venezuela in 1949.

In addition to "Desesperanza" she composed the songs "Como la primera vez", "Vente con el alba", "Noches de luna de Altamira", "Contigo", "Orquídeas azules" with lyrics by Mercedes Carvajal de Arocha (Lucila Palacios); "Luna de Camoruco", "La despedida", "Caribe" which was the theme of Radio Caracas Television for a long time; "La luz de mi ciudad", "El marinero", "No puedo olvidarte", "Canción de oro", "Sueño de Bolívar", "Paraguaná", "Curiana", "Orinoco", "Canción del aviador", "Siete lunas", "Siempre", "Aleluya", "Carnaval de candela", "Concierto sentimental", "Vals de concierto", "Petit suite", "Mi general Bolívar" and "Diez canciones sentimentales".[liv]

Felipe Pirela was the stage name used by the singer *Felipe Antonio Pirela Morón*, who was born in Maracaibo, on September 4, 1941, and died tragically in San Juan, Puerto Rico on July 2, 1972. On that date, the country celebrates the National Day of the Bolero.

From a very young age he showed his talent for music and when he was just 13 years old, together with two of his brothers and neighbors from the El Empedrao neighborhood of his hometown, he formed the group Los Happy Boys, which performed boleros by renowned singers such as Alfredo Sadel, Olga Guillot and Lucho Gatica.

In 1958 he was one of the first artists to perform on the Marabina radio station "Ondas del Lago", with a short presence on the radio spectrum. In July of that same year, he returned to Caracas and performed in nightclubs and on a television channel.

On his return to Maracaibo, he joined "Los Peniques". With this group he began as a professional recording only two songs on the only album produced by this group in 1960.

He began to become popular when he was hired by the musician, director and arranger of Dominican origin Billo Frómeta to be part of his famous orchestra as a bolero singer. He became so popular that Billo's radio program only received letters addressed to the young artist.

With the orchestra of such a renowned musician he recorded in 1961 as a soloist the album "Canciones de ayer y hoy", accompanied by the voices of Cheo García and Joe Urdaneta.

Outside of this group he traveled to Mexico, where he performed and recorded his first album entitled "Un Solo Camino: México". In that country he was proclaimed "The

Bolero of America". The album "Boleros con Guitarras" also appeared, the only one of its kind in his history.

Later he toured the United States, Colombia, Santo Domingo, Puerto Rico, Ecuador, Peru.

Luis Cruz was a composer, singer and guitarist who was born in Caracas on July 17, 1930, and died on the night of Saturday, April 22, 2012 in Cabudare, Lara State.

His inspiration is due the birth of one of the most popular songs in the country, "**Ay que noche tan preciosa**", present at all birthday parties, with worldwide rank in various versions.

His first interpreter was the trio "Los Latinos", under his leadership, which he composed at the request of a friend's girlfriend for his birthday.

Years later Emilio Arvelo asked to record it as a filler for one of his albums which, curiously, was the only song that hit.

He also composed, among other successful songs. "Dumbi dumbi"- "Desconfiada", with which classes of four are taught, due to the ease of its interpretation, "La luna y el toro", "Tibisay", which was both song and innovative rhythm, first instrumental, and then he wrote the lyrics for the singer Mario Suárez; "Lamento de una cascada", "Corosito", "Campesinita", "Sendero", "Las corocoras" and "Era ella", among many others.

Another of his contributions to the history of popular music in Venezuela was the creation, together with Gonzalo Peña and José Petit, of "Los Naipes", a group initially a trio and then a quartet, incorporating highly successful female voices such as Mirla Castellanos, Mirtha Pérez, Tania Salazar, Oly Monasterios, Milángela, Marlene Perdomo, Nilda López and Estelita del Llano.

He shared, among many other important national and international characters in the artistic world, with Renny Otolina, Alfredo Sadel, Canelita Medina, Lucho Gatica, Javier Solís, Elton John, "Los Cinco Latinos", Johnny Albino, Felipe Pirela, Cherry Navarro, Pedro Vargas, Carmen Delia Dippini, Virginia López, Bobby Capó, José Luis Rodríguez, Lila Morillo, "Los 007", "Los Dart", "Los Impala", Henry Stephen, María Teresa and Rosa Virginia Chacín, Mario Suárez, Mirla Castellanos, César Costa, José Feliciano, Andy Montañés, Oscar D'Leon, "Dimensión Latina", Alicia Plaza and "Los Hermanos Rodríguez".[lv]

Simón Díaz was the stage name of the composer, singer, musician and actor *Simón Narciso Díaz Márquez*, who was born in Barbacoas, Aragua State, on August 8, 1928 and died in Caracas on February 19, 2014.

He was known as "**Uncle Simon**."

He rescued the tonada llanera convinced that it is a musical air of unique characteristics, which is why he dedicated himself entirely to disseminating, studying and composing it until it became an authentic musical genre in which great artists such as Mercedes Sosa (Argentina), Caetano Veloso, Iván Lins y Joyce (Brazil), Joan Manuel Serrat (Spain), Danny Rivera, Ednita Nazario, Cheo Feliciano and Gilberto Santa Rosa (Puerto Rico) and Franco De Vita (Venezuela), among others.

He shared the stage with Mario Moreno "Cantinflas", Plácido Domingo, Lucho Gatica, Marco Antonio Muñiz, Joan Manuel Serrat, Mercedes Sosa, Atahualpa Yupanqui, among others. In addition, he was the first Venezuelan artist to perform at "Carnegie Hall" in New York

In 1998 he celebrated "The 50 years of Artistic Life".

His most internationally known work, the llanero passage "Caballo viejo", has been interpreted, among others, by Plácido Domingo, Ray Conniff, Julio Iglesias, Celia Cruz, Rubén Blades, Gilberto Santarrosa, Gipsy Kings, Tania Libertad, María Dolores Pradera, Armando Manzanero, Barbarito Diez, Richard Clayderman, Gipsy Kings, Juanes, among others, Ry Cooder, Martirio and Oscar de León.

This theme has more than 350 versions and has been translated into 12 languages.

In 1963 he recorded his first album, and since then he has recorded more than 70 volumes throughout his career as a singer and songwriter.

Artists of the stature of Mercedes Sosa, Joan Manuel Serrat, Danny Rivera, Ednita Nazario, Cheo Feliciano and Franco De Vita, as well as outstanding directors and composers of academic music managed to make their tunes acquire the universal character of a new musical genre.

In 2000, he released an album of boleros entitled "Amorosamente" in which he recalled songs that he sang in his beginnings as a bolero singer: "Noche de ronda", "Mujer", "Palabras de mujer", "Santa" and "Solamente una vez (Agustín Lara); " Write to me" (Guillermo Castillo Bustamante); "In Love with You (Rafael Hernández); " Unforgettable" (Julio Gutiérrez); "Para qué recordar" (María Grever); "Quiéreme mucho" (Gonzalo Roig), "El Ciego" (Armando Manzanero) and "Nunca" (Ricardo López Méndez/Augusto Cárdenas Pinelo).

Ítalo Pizzolante was a composer and musician who was born in Puerto Cabello, Carabobo State, on December 2, 1928, and died in Valencia on March 12, 2011.

His musical vocation began at home.

With the song **"Provincianita"** of his authorship, he was the winner of the First Venezuelan Music Contest of the

Central University of Venezuela where he graduated as a civil engineer.

He represented Venezuela in 1992 at the Havana Bolero Festival, where he won first place.

His best-known bolero, "Motivos", composed on December 1, 1965, as a dedication to some friends at a party, has been performed, among others, by "La Rondalla Venezolana", the "Trio Los Panchos", Chucho Avellanet, Armando Manzanero, Alfredo Sadel, Vicente Fernández and Luis Miguel.

Another of his boleros, "Mi Puerto Cabello", had Felipe Pirela as its first interpreter accompanied by Billo's Caracas Boys Orchestra.

On July 17, 1998, this song was declared the Official Anthem of Puerto Cabello.

René Rojas was a composer who was born in Campo Elías, Yaracuy State, on August 2, 1928, and died in Caracas, on March 9, 2000.

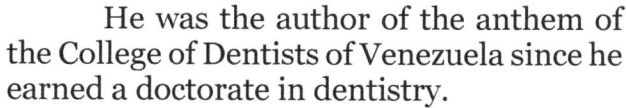

He was the author of the anthem of the College of Dentists of Venezuela since he earned a doctorate in dentistry.

At the age of 19 he composed his first bolero, "**Evocación**", which immediately became known in the voices of Eduardo Lanz and Mario Suárez.

On August 17, 1948, he met the tenor Alfredo Sadel, establishing a close and very professional friendship between them, which encouraged him to continue composing other popular songs.

This is how "Anoche te amé", "Solo en la noche", "Sufra mujer", "Alma pasional", "Clamor", "Déjame olvidar", "Repaso", "Luna callada", "De que vale decirlo", "En cualquier lugar", "Canto triste", "Canción de cuna para la tarde", "Chipolita mía", "Contemplación", "María Margarita", "Paisaje azul", "Mi niña de diez", "Vals para un niño", "A mi jardinera", "Un son para niños antillanos" were born. "Un bolero para el samán de Güere", "El gasero" and others.[lvi]

Héctor Cabrera was a singer and actor who was born in Caracas, on February 13, 1932, and died in the same city on June 8, 2003.

He was called *"The Golden Voice of Venezuela"* and *"The Poet of Song"*.

In 1949 he made his professional debut with Gerver Hernández's orchestra in "Radiodifusora Venezuela", continuing later in the programs "La Caravana Camel", "Desfile Chesterfield" and "Fiesta Fabulosa", on Radio Caracas, accompanied by Billo Frómeta.

In 1951 he made his first recordings with the group "Los Juancheros", of Clemente Robaina, sponsored by Polar beer, after triumphing in the musical program "Tribunal del Arte Popular", broadcast at the time by the Caracas "Radio Continente", with the accompaniment of the then young musician Aldemaro Romero, who would later be one of the great musical figures of the country with his first orchestra.

He was part of the musical group of Juan Vicente Torrealba y sus Torrealberos, where one of his hits was achieved with the song "Rosario". In Cuba he recorded for the Velvet label the Guarani song "El pájaro chogüi". which became the biggest hit of the time in all of Latin America.

Later he began an international tour that led him to perform on stages in Mexico, the United States and Europe and when he returned to Venezuela, he found himself recording the bolero "Acompáñame" as a duet with Mirtha Pérez.

In 1970 he won first place in the IV Song Festival in Buenos Aires, with the song "Las cosas que me alejan de ti".

He was the winner of the "First Festival of the Golden Voice of Venezuela" in 1969 in Barquisimeto.

He recorded more than a thousand songs for the labels Velvet, Sonus, RCA Víctor, Music Hall (Argentina), Discorona, Basf, Discomoda, Suramericana del Disco and Manoca, among others.[lvii]

Marco Tulio Maristany was a singer and guitarist who was born in Valencia, on April 25, 1916, and died in Caracas on May 28, 1984. Singer and guitarist.

He was part of the Trio Los Cantores del Trópico, with whom he traveled through much of Latin America and had his Trio Maristany.

He was an artist for RCA Victor, and Odeon in Argentina, among others. He also sang in the orchestras of Luis Alfonzo Larraín, Ulises Acosta, Luis María Billo Frómeta, Efraín Orozco and Aldemaro Romero and many others.

From 1952 to 1964 he maintained on Radio Caracas Radio the program "Canciones Bajo las Estrellas".

He popularized the boleros "Serenata", "Esclavo", "Una canción", "Cuando te veo a mi lado" and "Eclipse", among many others.[lviii]

Mario Suárez was the stage name of singer *Mario Enrique Quintero Suárez*, who was born in Maracaibo on January 19, 1926, and died in the same city on November 14, 2018.

He performed llanera music and boleros.

At a very young age he lived in Caracas, where he performed as a singer at fairs and amateur radio programs.

The Bolero in Latin America

In 1947 he signed his first recording contract with the American company "Coda Records Company" with which he recorded his first 78 rpm and 10-inch album, with the songs "Pena Goajira", by the Venezuelan composer José Reyna, and "Adiós" by the also Venezuelan musician Ángel Briceño.

Later he ventured with various musical groups in the country producing the recording of several boleros, among which "No me sigas mirando", composed by the orchestra director Luis Alfonzo Larrain, "Desesperación", by Guillermo Castillo Bustamante, and "Nocturnal", by José Mojica and José Sabre Marroquín.

With Aldemaro Romero and his orchestra he recorded, among others, the waltz "Morir es nacer", by Rafael Andrade and Manuel Rodríguez Cárdenas.

He popularized the songs "Mujer llanera", "Rosa Angelina", "Madrugada llanera", "Sabaneando", "El beso que te di", "Aquella noche", "Campesina", "Arpa", "Testigo de un romance", "Barquisimeto", "La potranca zaina", "La paraulata", "Atardecer larense", "Amores de mi tierra", "Luz de luna", "Desilusión", "Por el camino", "Nunca sabré", "Canta claro", "Nunca sabré", "Moliendo café", "Morir es nacer", "Ayúdame Dios mío", "Adiós", "Tu boca", "Nocturnal", "Desperation" and "Don't keep looking at me", among many others.

Rosa Virginia Chacín is a singer, economist and commercial administrator who was born in Caracas on June 9, 1940.

She is known as **"The Sweetest Voice in Venezuela"**

She began her musical activities in 1958 when the Venezuelan poet and composer José Enrique "Chelique"

Sarabia discovered his talent at a student event at the Central University of Venezuela.

She has performed live throughout Venezuela, through the radio and all the Venezuelan television stations and has  recorded dozens of full-length albums and compact discs. The beauty of her singing has also become known outside the Venezuelan borders, as an ambassador of our music.

Her first album was titled "Alma Juvenil", which was followed, among many others, by "Si te vas de mi", "Un momento contigo", "La voz más dulce de Venezuela" and "Mi propio yo".[lix]

María Teresa Chacín is a singer, producer, entertainer, cuatrista and psychologist who was born in Caracas on January 22, 1945.

 She has to her credit the recording of more than 50 albums of Venezuelan folklore and Latin American romantic between LP and CD formats accompanied by renowned musicians such as Juan Vicente Torrealba, Chelique Sarabia, Armando Manzanero, guitarist Rodrigo Riera and Aldemaro Romero when conducting the London Symphony Orchestra in one of her recordings.

She was the first Venezuelan to win a Latin Grammy Award.

Her career as a performer began in 1963 when she was part of the Orfeón Universitario de la Universidad Central de Venezuela, standing out for 8 years as a soloist.

On November 29, 1993, the Acoustic Shell of Anaco, Anzoátegui State, by unanimous decision of the Municipal

Chamber, was inaugurated with the name of "María Teresa Chacín Acoustic Shell" and on July 17, 2002, she was designated Guest of Honor of the Cocorote Municipality of the State of Yaracuy.

His discography includes, among many others, the albums "Canta para ti". "Todo me es igual", "María Teresa y sus éxitos", "Rosas en el mar" and "Canta con María Teresa".[lx]

Estelita del Llano is the stage name of singer and actress *Berenice Perrone Huggins*, who was born in Tumeremo, Bolívar State, on September 28, 1937.

She is known as "**The Queen of Bolero**", making herself known in a contest of "Radio Cultura", in Caracas.

She was a member of the quintet "Los Zeppys".

Among her greatest hits is a long-named bolero, "Tú sabes que te quiero y sabes que te adoro", arranged by Jhonny Quiroz that in her voice was reduced to "Tú sabes", recorded in 1963 with the RCA Victor label, the only star, then of that label.

"I would like to ask", "Who has your love", "This house", "Desperately" and "The journey", as well as "You know" are part of her repertoire that consecrated her.[lxi]

José Luis Rodríguez He is a singer, record producer, actor and businessman. who was born in Caracas on January 14, 1943.

He is known as "*El Puma*".

His beginnings as a singer occurred in the group of youth voices called "Los Zeppy", where he replaced vocalist Ariel Rojas.

His first solo album for the Venezuelan label "Velvet" in LP format entitled "Chelique Sarabia presents his new voice: José Luis Rodríguez" had little acceptance in the public.

In September 1963 he replaced the bolero singer Felipe Pirela in Billo's Caracas Boys Orchestra. There he stayed for four years performing boleros and occasionally Dominican merengue, Christmas music and cha-cha-chá, traveling through the Caribbean, Central and South America recording about 6 LPs and some singles, which consisted of 34 songs and 9 mosaics of various dance themes.

In September 2005 he presented the album "15 éxitos de José Luis Rodríguez", containing his most popular hits since the beginning of his internationalization, in new versions, backed by the American label Líderes Entertainment.

Also, among many others, he recorded the albums, "Voglio conquistarti", "El último beso", "Señora Bonita", "Homenaje a José Alfredo Jiménez", "Inolvidable", "Interpreta Manuel Alejandro", "Boleros de siempre" and "Dos clásicos".

THE AUTHOR

Eladio Rodulfo González, who signs his work in prose or verse with both surnames, was born in the village of Marabal, which later became the parish of the same name in the Mariño Municipality, Sucre State, Venezuela.

He was born on February 18, 1935. He has a degree in Journalism from the Central University of Venezuela, is a social worker, poet and cultural researcher.

In the first years of his life, he was a dependent in the warehouse of his father, an oil worker of the Creole Petroleum Corporation in Lagunillas, Zulia State, where he began high school at the Santa Rosa de Lima School, which he continued at the Alcázar and Juan Vicente González high schools and the National School of Social Work, both institutions located in Caracas. He was also co-founder of the Minors Division of the extinct Technical Corps of the Judicial Police and of the Nueva Esparta Section of the National College of Journalists, where he was a member of the board of directors in several secretariats and also chaired the Institute of Social Welfare for Journalists.

At the extinct School of Journalism of the Central University of Venezuela, later transformed into the School of Social Communication, on October 9, 1969, he obtained a degree in Journalism. Later he completed a postgraduate degree in Public Administration, mention Organization and Methods, and a course in Cultural Research Research. He also took police courses in Washington, D.C., and Fort Bragg, North Carolina.

Has published the following books:

I. Prose
-The disappearance of minors in Venezuela, quoted by Julio Cortázar in La vuelta al día en 80 mundos.
-The food problems of the Venezuelan minor.
-El Padre Gabriel.
-Colaboradores del gobernador.
-Margarita Moderna.
-Siempre Narváez.
-Margarita y sus personajes (5 vols.)
-Caracas sí es gobernable.
-Así se transformó Margarita.
-Breviario neoespartano.
-Patrimonio Cultural Mariñense.
-Festividades Patronales Mariñenses
-Manifestaciones culturales populares del Municipio Marcano.
-Festividades patronales del Municipio Villalba.
-Festividades patronales del Municipio Antolín del Campo.
-Manifestaciones culturales populares del Municipio Gómez.
-La mujer margariteña.
-Manifestaciones culturales populares de la Isla de Coche.
-El asesinato de Óscar Pérez
-El asesinato del Capitán de Corbeta Rafael Acosta Arévalo.
-El asesinato de Fernando Albán.
-Festividades Navideñas.
-Morel: Política y Gobierno.
-Niños maltratados.
-El deterioro de la salud en el socialismo del siglo XXI.
-Dos localidades del Estado Sucre.
-Háblame de Pedro Luis.
-Estado Nueva Esparta 1990-1994.

-Chávez no fue bolivariano.
-Rómulo Betancourt: Más de medio siglo de historia.
-Los ojos apagados de Rufo.
-Festividades patronales del Estado Nueva Esparta.
-La Hemeroteca Loca (6 volúmenes).
-Nuestra Señora de Los Ángeles, patrona de Los Millanes.
-Pelea de gallos.
-El gallo en el arte, la literatura y la cultura popular.
-Carlos Mata: luchador social.
-Vida y obra de Jesús Manuel Subero.
-Breviario Neoespartano.
-Cuatro periodistas margariteños.
-Francisco Lárez Granado El Poeta del Mar.
-Textos periodísticos escogidos (2 vols.).
-Cristo en la devoción religiosa católica neoespartana.
-La historia de Acción Democrática en tres reportajes periodísticos.
-La Virgen María en la devoción religiosa de Margarita y Coche.
-Festividades patronales del Municipio García del Estado Nueva Esparta, Venezuela.
-La guerra del dictador Nicolás Maduro contra comunicadores sociales y medios desde enero hasta mayo de 2018.
-La Quema del Año Viejo en América Latina.
-La Quema de Judas en Venezuela, 2013-2014.
-La Quema de Judas en Venezuela.
-La Quema de Judas en Venezuela, 2015.
-La Quema de Judas en Venezuela, 2016.
-La Quema de Judas en Venezuela (2017-2018).
-Catorce años de periodismo margariteño.
-Grandes compositores del bolero.
-Grandes intérpretes del bolero.
-El Bolero en América Latina.
-El Bolero en Venezuela.

-La guerra asimétrica del dictador Hugo Chávez contra comunicadores sociales y medios desde 1999 hasta 2009.
-La guerra asimétrica del dictador Nicolás Maduro contra comunicadores sociales y medios desde 2013 hasta 2014.
-Imprenta y Periodismo en Costa Rica.
-Gobernadores contemporáneos del Estado Nueva Esparta.
-Marabal de mis amores.
-Hemeroteca: Periodismo Moderno neoespartano.
-Historia de los primeros periódicos de América Latina.
-La libertad de prensa en Venezuela.
-Los indígenas en el socialismo del siglo XXI.
-La corrupción en el socialismo del siglo XXI (3 volumes).
-Los presos del narcodictador Nicolás Maduro (4 volumes).
-Morir en el socialismo del siglo XXI (5 volumes)
-La Barbarie Represiva de la Narcodictadura de Nicolás Maduro (5 volumes)
-La Diáspora en el Socialismo del Siglo XXI, Tomos I, II, III, IV and V

II. Poetry
-Antología Poética.
-Elegía a Juan Ramón Jiménez, ganador de un premio nacional de poesía convocado por el Liceo Andrés Bello, de Caracas
-Covacha de sueños.
- ¡Cómo dueles, Venezuela!
-A Briceida en Australia (tríptico).
-Elevación (tríptico).
-Divagaciones (tríptico).
-Nostalgia (tríptico).
-Entre sueños.

- Mosaicos Líricos.
- Elegía a mi hermana Alcides.
- Cien sonetillos.
- Alegría y tristeza.
- Encuentros y Extravíos.
- Ofrenda Lírica a Briceida.
- Guarumal.
- Primera Antología de poemas comentados y destacados.
- Segunda Antología de poemas comentados y destacados.
- Tercera Antología de poemas comentados y destacados.
- Brevedades Líricas.
- Cuarta Antología de poemas comentados y destacados.
- Poemas disparatados.
- La niña de Marabal.
- La niña de El Samán.
- Añoranza y otros poemas escogidos.
- Incógnita.
- Noche y otros poemas breves.
- Mis mejores poemas.
- Cuitas a la amada.
- Poesía Política.
- Poemas Políticos.

Página Web: cicune.org
Twitter: @mauritoydaniel
Email: cicune@gmail.com

References

[i] Sources: Ecured.cu and Wikipedia
[ii] Source: Wikipedia
[iii] Fuente: Wikipedia
[iv] Fuente: Wikipedia
[v] Sources: https://music.aple.com and Wikipedia
[vi] Source: http://sandritocubanito.blogspot.com
[vii] Source: https://ecured.cu
[viii] Source: https://ecured.cu
[ix] Source: Wikipedia
[x] Source: Wikipedia
[xi] Source: Wikipedia
[xii] Source: Wikipedia
[xiii] Source: Wikipedia
[xiv] Source: Wikipedia
[xv] Source: Wikipedia
[xvi] Source: https://ecured.cu
[xvii] Source: Wikipedia
[xviii] Sources: Ecured and Wikipedia
[xix] Source: Wikipedia
[xx] Source: Wikipedia
[xxi] Source: Wikipedia
[xxii] Source: Mario Zaldívar. Costa Ricans in Music
[xxiii] Source: Radio ACAM
[xxiv] Source: Radio ACAM
[xxv] Source: http://www.canara.org/component/content/article/903-panorama/capsulas/592-jorge-duarte.
[xxvi] Source: https://www.culturacr.net/los-10-grandes-boleros-costarricenses/
[xxvii] Sources: El Comercio, El Universo, Wikipedia
[xxviii] Source: Wikipedia
[xxix] Sources: El Blog del Bolero, Wikipedia
[xxx] Sources: Jesús Rincón Murcia, text on the Web of June 4, 1991. Wikipedia.

https://www.radionacional.co/noticia/musica/
https://borradopedia.com/index.php
https://narinoacf.blogspot.com
https://caracol.com.co/radio

[xxxi] Source: Pedro Delgado Malagón. "El bolero dominicano de 1930 a 1960". http://www.elcaribe.com, 28 de enero de 2014.

Gustavo Olivo Peña. "Maestro Papa Molina, un dominicano grande entre los grandes". Acento, 29 de septiembre de 2011.

Wikipedia, la enciclopedia libre.

Historia Dominicana en Gráficas, 18 de agosto de 2017.

[xxxii] Sources: Editorial Digitsl La Estrella. The Musical Stinger Blog. Of Music and something else

[xxxiii] Sources: Edwin Ricardo Pitre Vásquez. "The Panamanian Bolero Poetry and Feeling", https://www.academia.edu

"Panama will have its Bolero festival." La Prensa, April 17, 2002.

[xxxiv] Source: Gloria Acosta, March 28, 2019

[xxxv] Source: Wikipedia

[xxxvi] Source: Wikipedia

[xxxvii] Source: Wikipedia

[xxxviii] Sources: http://adiolakalle.pe/los-hermanos-castro. https://www.facebook.com

[xxxix] Sources: Peruvian Association of Authors and Composers. The Bolero Corner

[xl] Source: Wikipedia

[xli] Source: https://larepublica.pe

[xlii] Source: Peruvian Association of Authors and Composers.

[xliii] Source: Wikipedia

[xliv] Source: https://www.last.fm/es/music/Charlie+Figueroa https://acme-cali.jimdo.com/puerto-rico/charlie-figueroa/

[xlv] Source: http://www.kooltouractiva.com

[xlvi] Source: https://prpop.org/biografias/virginia-lopez/

[xlvii] Source: http://dawn.over-blog.es/article-rafael-mu-oz-y-su-orquesta.

[xlviii] Source: http://triosmusicales.tripod.com/triosprincipalespr.htm

[xlix] Source: http://amatitlanesasi.blogspot.com

Pablo Juárez. "The singer César de Guatemala, author and interpreter of Mi Plegaria, dies." Prensa Libre, December 27, 2018.

[l] Sources: direcciondelasartes.blogspot.com.

https://wikiguate.com.gt/coro-nacional-de-guatemala/

[li] Sources: "Fundandora de las Voces Blancas Elisa Soteldo died". *Correo del Orinoco*, 23 January, 2016 12:38.

Venezuela and History, January 21, 2017.

[lii] Source: https://melomanoincurable.wordpress.com.

http://cantoliricovenezolan.wix.com.

www.eglycolinamarin.com.

http://cantoliricovenezolan.wix.com.

[liii] Sources: cancionescribeme.blogspot.com. Wikipedia

[liv] Source: orinocopadrerio.blogspot.com
venciclopedia.com/index.php?title=María_Luisa_Escobar
   Wikipedia
[lv] Source: https://elblogdelbolero.wordpress.com/
[lvi] Source: www.sacven.org.
[lvii] Source: http://www.musica.com.
www.emol.com.
www.ucla.edu.ve.
https://elblogdelbolero.wordpress.com.
http://elultimoromanticoradio.blogspot.com
[lviii] Source: Venezuela and History, May 27, 2018.
Orinoco Padre Río.
[lix] Source: http://orinocopadrerio.blogspot.com.
      www.rosavirginiachacin.com.
      http://barraezo.blogspot.com.
[lx] Sources: El Nacional.com.
música.com.
Wikipedia
[lxi] Sources: buenamusica.com
elblogdelbolero.wordpress.com

www.ingramcontent.com/pod-product-compliance
Lightning Source LLC
LaVergne TN
LVHW052245070526
838201LV00113B/352/J